W9-DES-461

11/17/0

My Greatest Race

My Greatest Race

by twenty of the finest motor racing drivers of all time

edited by Adrian Ball
for the Jim Clark Foundation

E. P. Dutton & Co., Inc.   New York   1974

CONTENTS

ACKNOWLEDGMENTS

The illustrations in this book are reproduced by kind permission of the following: those on pages 1, 130, Keystone Press; pages 2, 57, 111, London Art Tech; 3, 35, 45, 90, 92, 126, Publifoto Milan; page 6, Central Press Photos Ltd; pages 13, 48, 66, 102, 118, 123, 134, 137, 139, Ford of Britain; pages 15, 18, 49, *Motor*; page 24, Agence Rol; pages 26, 30, 75, 97, 98, 116, *Autosport*; pages 33, 125, Montagu Motor Museum; pages 39, 41, Bondera A Scacchi; page 43, Motorphoto Studio Werner Eisele; pages 50, 62, 108, Geoffrey Goddard; pages 53, 70, 76, 78, 80, 81, 103, 104, 107, 135, Phipps Photographic; pages 60, 65, 73, 86, 107, 121, *Autocar*; page 61, London Express; pages 82, 83, 85, Van Beuer Brussels; page 89, Camera Press; pages 110, 112, Klemantaski; page 129, MB-Fotodienst; page 132, Mercedes-Benz.

INTRODUCTION
by Adrian Ball

This collection of motor-racing stories spread over four decades has been a remarkable labour of love for men and women working in four continents. Everyone connected with *My Greatest Race* – contributors, photographers, researchers, and the editor – has given his or her services without fee. Many books are described as unique. Quite apart from the fact that no previous book of this nature has been produced, the voluntary support we have received must make *My Greatest Race* qualify for the 'unique' accolade.

The object of this unstinted voluntary effort by twenty drivers who have been household names at one time or another for fifty years is the Jim Clark Foundation. This international charitable trust fund was established as a significant and lasting memorial to Jim Clark, OBE, twice World Champion Motor Racing Driver, who was killed in a race at Hockenheim, West Germany, in April 1968. The Foundation promotes and assists research into motoring safety, both on the road and on the racing track. Among its major projects of benefit to race drivers have been investigations into aerofoils on racing cars and the properties of fire-resistant clothing, a full-scale study of motor cycle safety, and a detailed analysis of the causes of all Grand Prix accidents between 1966 and 1972.

There are, happily, many organisations throughout the world concerned with road safety in one form or another. The Jim Clark Foundation, though involved in all aspects of safety on two, three, and four wheels, has naturally a particularly soft spot for motor sport, and the world's drivers have come increasingly to appreciate this fact. The two investigations into the qualities of fire-resistant clothing, published in 1971 and 1972, were warmly received by racing drivers everywhere and quickly became reference books for manufacturers and retailers.

It was therefore with a feeling of confidence, as Administrative Secretary of the Foundation, that I began inviting past and present drivers to contribute to this book during the summer of 1971. I cannot say that the literary response was immediate (the text took almost two years to assemble!) but from the outset there was no doubt that the top drivers of this generation, and of the previous generation, would do their utmost to make *My Greatest Race* the best possible fund-raising vehicle for the Foundation. Generous pledges of help came without delay, even though in some cases strenuous racing programmes and globe-trotting delayed for months the actual delivery of copy (and kept the world's telegraph and cable offices fully employed in the interim!).

My request to drivers was a simple one: to recall in their own words their 'greatest races' — which did not necessarily mean their most spectacular victories. I went to drivers whose careers stretched back to the 1920s, as well as to the circuit champions of the 1970s, because I felt this would enhance the appeal of the book, even to the youngest readers. I hoped for variety, drama, humour, and philosophy in the stories — and was not disappointed in any of these fields. Without prompting from myself, or communication between themselves, the contributors submitted a remarkably well-balanced collection of stories dating from 1930. There was need for only limited editorial support, so my task as editor was far from onerous. No Fleet Street 'ghosts' stalk through these pages, and I trust that readers with experience of motor-racing books will soon come to realise this!

It was perhaps inevitable that a large minority of our drivers should have chosen to write about those fantastic and gruelling marathons, the Mille Miglia and the Le Mans 24 Hour Race. We had five contributions with recollections of the 1000-mile Italian classic, from Count 'Johnny' Lurani's story of his 1933 drive in a British MG to Piero Taruffi's account of what was both the last Mille Miglia and his own farewell to the sport. Two chapters recall the flavour of Le Mans, in the contributions by Innes Ireland (1959) and Jacky Ickx describing the event as it appeared to him ten years later. By a happy chance, we also have eye-witness reports on those much-loved circuits, the long-dead Brooklands and the ever-exciting Indianapolis. Our coverage is completed by stories about eight national Grand Prix events. No editor unable to specify subjects in advance could have been more fortunate in the random choices of his contributors.

Racing drivers have their favourites among the circuits so it is inevitable that some should link their greatest races with the venues in which they were happiest and most at home. Two of our drivers, for instance, recall Monaco with great affection. Jack Brabham says in recalling his first big Grand Prix victory, in 1959: 'That sunny day in Monte Carlo is something I shall never forget.' He admits to having had a soft spot for the round-the-houses circuit during his entire career, although he did not win there again, despite his great effort to succeed in 1970. Graham Hill is similarly devoted to Monaco, partly because the race began in the year of his birth. Hill recalls his 1965 victory by the Mediterranean as 'one of the best races I have ever run, or ever won'. That completed a personal hat-trick and, he writes, 'it really put a glow in me. I don't think I have ever felt quite like it before. A tremendous feeling of peace, serenity, and fulfilment . . .'

Jackie Stewart, on the other hand, selects a circuit which he has always approached with some dread: the Nurburgring. In stark contrast to the Brabham and Hill memories of duelling in the sun at Monte Carlo, Stewart remembers winning a race in appalling conditions, an event he expected, and hoped, to be stopped on every lap. Many drivers say in interviews that Nurburgring is their most satisfying or favourite circuit but, in Stewart's view, those comments are so often made in the comfort of an armchair. Whenever the flying Scot returns to the pits of the German circuit he takes a deep breath because, 'My God, I'm pleased to be home!' Stewart's account of his 1968 German Grand Prix victory, in miserable fog and a steady drizzle, suggests that sometimes a man's greatest race is one from which he derives not pleasure but heartfelt relief at having triumphed, and survived, against all the odds.

There is perennial interest, sometimes sentimental, sometimes censorial, in the attitude to the sport of the wives of the top drivers. We present two 'greatest races' in which the feelings of the driver's wife were paramount. Philippe Etancelin was determined not to drive in the 1930 French Grand Prix, but his wife submitted his name without his knowledge. In very different vein, Piero Taruffi entered the 1957 Mille Miglia with a solemn promise to his wife that it would be his very last race. Woman's ambivalent attitude to motor sport is illustrated neatly and simply in these two narratives. Etancelin at the time was more interested in his business of supplying wool for mattresses and goose and duck feathers for pillows, bolsters, and eiderdowns. While he slaved over his accounts, Mme Etancelin took the uncharacteristic course of submitting his name to the French Automobile Club and he eventually consented to enter the Grand Prix of that year at Pau. In the event, he became the first independent driver to win the French classic, driving a Bugatti which crossed the post with only a wine-glass of petrol in the tank. Taruffi, on the other hand, had promised his wife that the day he triumphed in the Mille Miglia he would give up racing. He describes

in these pages how he won the race, the goal of his life, and was then taken on one side by the legendary Enzo Ferrari and told quietly: 'I beg of you to remember your promise to your wife . . .'

National pride is a strong sentiment in most drivers, and five of our contributors have chosen races in which their triumph is of particular pleasure to them because of the prestige it brought their country at the time. Perhaps the most remarkable is Baron Huschke von Hanstein's account of the 1940 Mille Miglia, a race staged when Europe was at war and motor sport was about to be forgotten for half a decade. It was a matter of enormous prestige for a German car to win, and von Hanstein duly took the laurels for his country. His story is particularly memorable because it recalls the great friendship at the time of German and French drivers who were supposed to be enemies but who could fraternise in still neutral Italy. I will always remember it because of the characteristically generous gesture von Hanstein made to his young co-driver, Walter Baumer. On instructions, von Hanstein drove his BMW for nearly all the 1000 miles; then, on an impulse, he handed over the wheel to Baumer to complete the last few miles and enjoy the thrill of crossing the line first. Von Hanstein never regretted his gesture — it was the last race for Baumer who was killed in the fighting soon afterwards.

Count 'Johnny' Lurani tells the story of how an Anglo-Italian team, sporting both the Union Jack and his own national flag on the bonnet of an MG, won an epic class victory in the 1933 Mille Miglia. Stirling Moss matches this with a graphic description of the same race twenty-two years later when he became the first overall British winner of the event. Baron de Graffenried acknowledges that a British driver should have won the first British Grand Prix, staged at Silverstone in 1949. But national prestige and luck do not always go hand in hand and we have the Baron's own warm account of how he took the chequered flag in a Maserati, a Swiss driver in an Italian car. He recalls his exultation at the time: 'It was my first victory in an international Grand Prix. I was the first Swiss ever to win such a race, and it was the very first British Grand Prix . . .'

Another tale of a reluctant entrant to a race who subsequently triumphed comes from Paul Frere, writing about the 1956 Belgian Grand Prix. In that year Frere, a journalist, was 'rationing' his drives to Jaguars as he wanted to serve the British marque exclusively. He had no intention of entering a Formula One event and consented reluctantly to handle a Ferrari after pressure from friends and the Italian stable. But Frere, the amateur last-minute entrant, drove his greatest race in coming second to Peter Collins and writes with pride that it remains the best placing achieved by a Belgian driver in his national Grand Prix. National pride of the present decade is described with feeling by Emerson Fittipaldi in his account of the 1973 Argentine Grand Prix. It was his first Grand Prix since he became World Champion and 10,000 of his compatriots were in Buenos Aires for the race. All South America was craving a win for the continent against the crack European drivers. That duel in the torrid heat, against the background of local political unrest, was 'the most difficult race of my life. The cars and drivers were so evenly matched at the head of the field that I am proud to have won in such company.'

The circuit is the dominant theme of three of our stories. No account of an Indianapolis event can ever be dull, but Mario Andretti's story of his great win in 1969, after failing twice, is surely one of the most graphic tales ever told about the brickyard. Andretti regards it as his greatest race, not because of the fifteen records he piled up in averaging nearly 157 miles an hour and grossing 206,000 dollars, but because it was the personal achievement of his life . . . 'I had climbed the mountain. I had conquered Indy.' In similar vein, Denny Hulme tells the saga of his six-year effort to win the South African Grand Prix. Between 1967 and 1971 he filled every place from second to sixth, but the chequered flag eluded him until 1972. He writes with supreme satisfaction: 'After six years of trying and so nearly getting there in two races, I felt there was some justice in motor racing after all!'

Luck is an element of many motor-racing victories and Juan Manuel Fangio acknowledges this in writing about the Italian Grand Prix of 1953. His best and worst experiences were at Monza; his serious crash there in 1952 was followed by a run of ill-luck which persisted until his magnificent victory on the Italian circuit the following year. Since Monza 1953, Fangio declares, he has always been aware that although a motor-racing driver must have all the skills, iron will, and nerves of steel, 'if he does not have luck he will not win races'. When two men duel for 260 miles and cross the line with only a second between them the winner must surely say: 'I'm a lucky man.' Raymond Mays tells us how it felt to be the driver who finished one second behind (to Prince Bira) in a wonderful account of the most dramatic race ever staged on the much-loved Brooklands circuit. Fate was doubly kind to Bira that day — seconds after he crossed the line his gearbox collapsed.

If luck can win a race, so can anger, as Olivier Gendebien admits in a very frank recollection of the 1956 Mille Miglia. Despite advance requests to the factory, his Ferrari 250 GT Saloon was far from watertight, an uncomfortable car to drive and handle. Gendebien says he competed in that event with a total lack of habitual respect for machines. He pushed the car to its limits, braking suddenly, crashing the gears brutally in his rage. He confessed: 'I was harsh and imprudent.' But his anger put him in a position of strength, with an utter determination to triumph in spite of the disadvantages. Gendebien won the Grand Touring category that year because of his angry determination to wring the very last drop of speed out of his battle-scarred Ferrari. And he observes that, no doubt, Enzo Ferrari's success sometimes depended on his ability to make his drivers grit their teeth and say, 'I'll show him!'

Froilan Gonzales says he has forgotten many of the races in his illustrious career, but 'always fresh in my mind is 14 July 1951'. His epic victory in the British Grand Prix is told with great humour and the reader will be delighted with the Gonzales dialogues with himself during the race. In the early laps: 'Pepito, you a peasant have entered a high society party.' As he fought for the lead: 'Pepito, what are you doing among so many Field Marshals?' When things got tough: 'Pepito, how will you get out of this?' And then, when victory was in sight, a triumphant: 'Pepito, you are ahead of the Field Marshals!'

Not all of our drivers could select just one 'greatest race'. For Innes Ireland, his whole career was 'great', in the sense that he enjoyed every minute of it; but he singles out several races for special mention, including the 1961 Solitude Grand Prix in which he drove a Lotus in the company of Jim Clark and just beat Jo Bonnier to the flag. Roy Salvadori similarly has various races to recall and talks about the great cars of his time, especially the Aston Martin and Cooper Monaco marques. He is one of those drivers who will always have a soft spot for the Goodwood circuit of the 1950s. 'Give me the recollection of a car and a competition at Goodwood on an English summer's day and you can keep the rest of the world.'

No driver can compete for long on the world's circuits without becoming something of a philosopher, and the contribution by Jacky Ickx probably sums up the reaction of many of our contributors when asked to recall their 'greatest race'. Ickx writes a penetrating study of the meaning of a victory: 'It depends what a fine victory means. In the early stages of his racing career a driver is only aware of the time-keeper's win. It is the only thing in which he is interested. But later, when he is able to strike a distinction between merit and the result, and when he realises that they do not always go hand in hand — far from it — he comes to prefer the former to the latter. This is easily explained as a victory one has deserved but not won, is more real than the victory won without being deserved. So it is logical for a driver to be really happy and fully satisfied with himself on some days when he has not won . . .'

The Jim Clark Foundation wishes to thank all the drivers who have given so much time and effort to making this book possible. It intends to devote royalties earned to further research aimed at making motor sport safer for both participants and spectators. As editor, I am personally indebted to all our distinguished contributors for their co-operation, usually at vast distances, in a project which in its earliest stages was a speculative venture which might never have seen the light of day. All the photographs in this book have been supplied to the Foundation without copyright fees. I am happy to acknowledge with thanks the invaluable support of the libraries of *Motor*, *Autocar*, the National Motor Museum, the British Leyland Motor Corporation and Ford of Britain; together with loans of prints by Louis Klemantaski, Geoffrey Goddard, and John Pillar. Other photographs were supplied by our contributors. Some of the stories have appeared in part elsewhere and thanks are due to Messrs William Kimber (publishers of *Life at the Limit* by Graham Hill) and Temple Press (publishers of *Works Driver* by Piero Taruffi). Several colleagues have assisted in research and organising work and I am indebted here to Michael Dineen, Douglas Merritt, Diana Hambling, and Jennifer Long. All have played a part in the international effort which has brought *My Greatest Race* to the starting grid.

London

1
Juan Manuel Fangio

ITALIAN GRAND PRIX 1953

Monza provides me with one of my worst as well as one of my best recollections of motor-racing. Worst because it was at Monza in June 1952 that I crashed and suffered injuries which kept me idle for six months. Best because the following year – after the most frustrating season of my career – I drove at Monza again in the Italian Grand Prix.

I returned to motor-racing in January 1953 full of optimism, full of the will to win. The old competitive spirit which always made me need to come first was, I thought, as active as ever; especially after six long months away from the circuits. But, in spite of my enthusiasm, I did not win a single race. I came second several times but finishing on top eluded me. And my lack of

Fangio during the 1953 Italian Grand Prix; his car
is number 50, and he is being led by Farina and
Ascari.

Opposite: Fangio leading Farina and Ascari at
Monza.

success coincided with a thoroughly bad season for Maserati so that by September we all of us needed a win very badly.

The 1953 Italian Grand Prix at Monza had a significance for me that few races have had. I needed to rehabilitate myself after the 1952 Monza disaster. For I was clearly still suffering the after-effects. I needed also to rehabilitate myself in the eyes of my employers, Maserati. But above all these considerations, it was important to me to regain the confidence of my mechanics who always worked with such devotion and dedication. These were the men we relied on for success on the day of the race. They spent sleepless nights preparing the cars for practice and for the races and yet still worked with tremendous speed in the pits whenever an emergency occurred during races.

One way or another my approach to this particular race was over-anxious and my confidence was not improved during the practice session when I was asked to test Marimon's Maserati because he had said he found it unstable. I learned that the car did not 'hold' and the lesson was a costly one. I was negotiating a curve at 130 mph when one of the rear tyres burst due to overstretching of the ply. This sent Marimon's car off the track backwards. It crashed through some bushes and although I got away with only a few painful bruises, I was very shaken. Many people said later that the Maserati — even with the new radius arms at the back — lacked the road-holding of the Ferraris in the curves, although it had the edge on them for speed in the straight.

The only good which seemed to come out of the practice day was the fact that I earned a place on the front row of the grid by lapping very fast indeed. Ascari had the fastest practice time but my own speed was only half a second slower than his 114·86 mph. The confidence that this might have given me was dissipated, however, by the spin off the track in Marimon's Maserati.

The Grand Prix race itself was extraordinarily demanding. There was no let-up during the whole of the 312 miles from start to finish. Each lap was just under 4 miles and for the first half of the first lap I was engulfed after a poor start. But I noted that Marimon's Maserati flashed into the lead on the return straight. He was passed almost immediately by Ascari in the Ferrari. In that first lap Ascari, Marimon, Farina and I were all bunched together barely 3 seconds apart. We swept round in each other's slipstream or hub-to-hub for lap after lap. The lead changed frequently. I would have it, then Ascari who would surrender it to Farina. I think the spectators had their share of thrills. The race was so close, our skills and nerve and the power of our cars were all evenly matched on the very fast Monza circuit.

Monza, by the way, is shaped like an automatic pistol with the barrel representing the long straight where the Grandstand faces the pits. We were achieving speeds of up to 160 mph along here, often wheel-to-wheel and so close that it was hardly surprising a certain amount of accidental shunting took place!

At 5 laps I was lying third to Ascari and Marimon; at 20 laps I was third to Ascari and Farina; at 40 laps I was second to Ascari with Marimon behind me; at 50 I had the lead with Ascari second and Farina third; at 60 Ascari was back in the lead again with Farina second and me third, and at 70 Ascari still led but I had got back to second place again, ahead of Farina. During all these exchanges I do not suppose we were more than half a second apart. We should all have been able to share the accolade at the end of 80 such momentous laps.

But as it happened the decision as to who would win this exhausting race was taken by Lady

4

Luck herself on the final lap. Farina was a little behind Ascari with me in third place. Farina held off braking when he approached the last but one bend only a few seconds before the end of the race.

He wanted maximum speed to take Ascari in one last bid to win. Farina went wide as he cornered and I took advantage of this to sneak into second place. Ascari, who stood between me and the victory I needed so badly, took the final curve very sharply and his Ferrari did a half spin. He was hit by Marimon. Farina, whom I had only just over-taken and was breathing down my neck, had to swerve to avoid hitting them. In that split second of danger I was through, winning literally in the 312th mile of a 312-mile race. In effect Ascari and Farina handed victory to me on a plate. Ascari had only a bruised back. Farina, not unnaturally, lost his temper and Marimon cut a cheek. I was speechless with surprise and joy.

Signor Lugo, the Maserati director, and Signor Orsi, the owner of the Maserati factory, to say nothing of the mechanics in the pit, were all wild with excitement. But often since that tense and ruthless battle with Ascari, Farina and Marimon, I have realised that a motor-racing driver may have all the skills — an iron will and nerves of steel — but if he does not have luck he will not win races.

2
Count Giovanni ('Johnny') Lurani

MILLE MIGLIA
1933

Even if in my long racing career I had lots of thrills, and many happy moments, undoubtedly my 'greatest race' was the 1933 Mille Miglia in which I drove with George Eyston the MG Magnette which won its class at a record speed and finished first in that great race.

At the end of March, the English team met in Milan. The cars and mechanics had come over from England to Genoa by the s.s. *Florentine* and then by road to Milan. The drivers had travelled overland and the team's headquarters were set up at the Hotel Continental. The three MGs for the race gave the impression of being magnificently prepared and finished, and seemed to be in perfect trim.

The cars were painted green with a little Union

Jack on each side and the one which Eyston and I were to drive had also an Italian flag painted on it in my honour. Lord Howe's car had, in addition, a blue and silver band (his own racing colours) painted on it.

Hugh McConnell soon took over the organisation with great energy and we started serious trials. The cars were lodged in the Traversi garage, then situated in the centre of Milan, and the British team was accompanied by a large number of journalists, technical men, and fans. I was the only member of the team with experience of the Mille Miglia and tried to instruct my companions and the mechanics on the peculiarities of the great competition. Being used to English races on closed circuits, they could not be persuaded that we had to go flat-out on normal roads, more or less free from traffic, and through towns and villages full of people who did not seem to get out of the road until the very last moment!

We had a great deal of trouble in finding the most suitable fuel and after several sorties with the cars we made our final preparations. The pre-selective change – although somewhat heavy and in the way – gave considerable advantages in a race like the Mille Miglia, particularly if one had a good knowledge of the route, but it was absolutely necessary to be accustomed to it to avoid unpleasant surprises!

A few days before the race, we went to Brescia for the scrutineering, and the presentation of our green MGs followed by the powerful Mercedes SS.KK created a great impression. The drawing of numbers went against me and I found myself obliged to go ahead of my team-mates and (as in 1932) ahead of our most powerful rival, Beppe Tuffanelli, twice winner and record holder of the 1100-cc class in the Mille Miglia, who was driving a 4-cylinder Maserati – a car with, as I knew by experience, brilliant characteristics! In addition to

the unfortunate draw, Eyston and I were given No 39 (three times 13) so that the horoscope was far from favourable, but, happily, I have never been superstitious!

We spent the eve of the race in Brescia, very enthusiastic and wide awake, and on the morning of 8 April we were ready to start. George Eyston was driving and I, still wearing my blood-red Alfa overalls for luck, was beside him. We left at 8.03. 'Tim' Birkin and Rubin followed 2 minutes later, Lord Howe with Hamilton 3, and Tuffanelli-Bertocchi 4 minutes later – so we had to play the fox!

By way of precaution, Eyston had fitted the car with rather soft sparking plugs as he feared the fouling of hard ones. He would not believe it was possible to maintain for long stretches the maximum speed of which our small cars were capable. So, after less than 5 km the engine started to lose speed and we had to stop and change all the six plugs! It was not a wonderful beginning!

As we were finishing the change, we heard the approaching sound of another car and just as we were starting off again Birkin's MG shot past at 160 km/h. George Eyston, in addition to being the holder of records on tracks all over the world, was a marvellous road driver and he soon succeeded in getting near Birkin, and so we went on in company until Bologna. For about 200 km there was just 20 or 30 metres between the two cars – several times Eyston overtook Birkin and went ahead and was in turn overtaken. It was a most exciting duel, at over 160 km/h, with the engine going like a turbine at 6000 rpm.

Eyston had the advantage of having a companion well acquainted with the road. In fact, in his memoirs he states: 'I relied implicitly on the guidance of my partner in the car, Johnny Lurani. With his right arm round my back, hanging on

7

to a strap fixed on the body, he would signal with the left, pointing this way and that.'

While we were going alongside Birkin the chase was well on, and Lord Howe's large Mercedes (No 95 in the race) had also left with all the spare parts to be used in case of damage during the race. It was driven by Penn Hughes, a very pleasant English driver who soon became a good friend and driving companion of mine, and he was accompanied by Lord Howe's mechanic. The last of the 98 competitors to leave was the great Tazio Nuvolari.

The first to reach Bologna was Borzacchini in an Alfa Romeo 8-cylinder at 161·8 km/h. Birkin was first of the 1100-cc class in 1 hour 28 minutes 35 seconds at the fantastic average of 141·01 km/h. Lord Howe followed in 1 hour 30 minutes 10 seconds, and we were at 20 seconds distance with an average of 139 km/h. We had taken exactly 50 seconds more than I had taken in 1932 with Canavesi in my Alfa Romeo 1500-cc.

It goes without saying that if we had not had to stop and change the plugs we would have been at the head of our class, but in spite of all we were in a very good position, and Tuffanelli, who was our most dangerous rival with his powerful Maserati, was a quarter of an hour behind and could be considered out of the race. Birkin had beaten the existing record by 12 minutes, and the average had jumped from 123 km/h to 141, and more!

At the Bologna control Birkin went on driving while Eyston and I changed places. After my experience in 1932 it had been decided that I should take over the wheel at Bologna and drive the most mountainous stretch of the route through the Raticosa and Futa Passes, and the Radicofani and Somma Passes to Perugia. These were sections of the route where the man at the wheel counted a great deal. I was fully trained for this important stretch and, in fact, began the uphill run near Lojano at full speed. Just outside Bologna the car

of some reckless spectator cut across the road and I had to do some real acrobatics to miss it. Eyston hung on desperately to the car, expecting the inevitable, but we managed to avoid it by a miracle. We went on at full speed and soon we overtook Birkin again. We were obliged to stop a couple of times to change plugs and each time Birkin went ahead of us, but a little later we found him engaged on the same task and so his advantage was cancelled and we began once more our exciting duel.

Thus we arrived near Florence and the contest became more and more exciting. The downhill stretch from Pratolino was done at a frightening speed, going at over 160 km/h, just missing the pavement and walls, and we reached the Viale dei Colli side by side. On the ultimate curve before the Piazzale Michelangelo I managed to get ahead of 'Tim' and arrived at the control with a 10-metre advantage. The officials were waiting ready to stamp our books, but when they saw us arriving like a shot, sliding to a stop with the wheels locked by the last-minute application of the brakes, they got in a panic and jumped all over the place.

During this chaos and confusion Birkin managed to get off! Now he was about 20 seconds ahead of us but I overtook him again and we renewed our duel at full speed.

At the control in Florence Birkin was still first at an average of 107 km/h in 2 hours 56 minutes beating the previous record by as much as 19 minutes. Eyston and I were second in 2 hours 58 minutes, ahead of Lord Howe. I had made the best time for our class from Bologna to Florence in 1 hour 28 minutes 7 seconds. This was just 4 seconds less than the time Canavesi and I had taken in the previous Mille Miglia.

Towards S. Casciano and farther on, on the road to Siena, our hard fight with Birkin, which lasted for nearly 400 km, was as closely contested as ever, but at last Birkin's MG started to belch forth clouds of smoke and slowed right down. We flashed past into the lead, encouraged by a cheery wave from Birkin.

In the Florence–Siena section we had taken 44 minutes 18 seconds and were seventh best time in the general classification among the 98 competitors, and Lord Howe, who was second in our class, had taken 32 seconds more. Our first supply depot was alongside the walls of Siena, and was directed by Bert Denly, the tiny English motor-cycle champion who afterwards became a specialist in long-distance records with Eyston. We had planned carefully the location of our depots and, in view of the capacity of our tanks, we had managed with three supply stations instead of the four which we had organised previously for the Alfra Romeo. At Siena the MG was refuelled, the brakes adjusted, we had a wash, drank some orangeade, and hurriedly stowed away sandwiches and bananas.

Just as we were starting off again, poor Birkin arrived slowly in a cloud of smoke. One look was enough to convince me that our friend was out of the race for good. His engine had given way under the tremendous strain put on it during our prolonged duel, whereas I, knowing the route better than Birkin, had managed to save the engine more than he could do while keeping up the infernal pace.

After Siena and towards Buonconvento, San Quirico, and Radicofani we continued to pass many of the cars which had left before us. On the downhill stretch of Radicofani we came on the extraordinary spectacle of a Fiat Balilla lying upside down in a field alongside the road, and minus both front wheels; then after a couple of curves we came to the entire front part of the upturned car lying in the middle of the road. It had

been projected there by the terrific impact, but miraculously the drivers were not seriously injured.

Our run towards Rome continued with the MG motoring splendidly. We reached the control, which, as usual, was situated at the Ponte Milvio, among the very first competitors, and got quite a reception. Greetings from friends whom we could not identify during the brief stop had to be returned collectively by a wave of the hand! At Rome, Eyston and I were solidly established in first place in our class in 6 hours 16 minutes 30 seconds, and fifteenth in the whole race. We had beaten Tuffanelli's previous record by 24 minutes and gained as much as 20 minutes on Lord Howe, who was second in our class, while everyone else was far behind. In the general classification, Borzacchini was still in the lead at record speed, followed by Nuvolari, Cortese, and Taruffi.

The stretch from Rome to Terni was particularly suited to our small car and everything felt magnificent; the road was perfect, the weather good, and the car 'going like a bomb'. What a thrill it was to be first and to be driving with confident daring nearer to the finish. I took 59 minutes 53 seconds from Rome to Terni at 98·28 km/h, a time beaten only by Nuvolari, who in the meantime had taken command of the race after the withdrawal of Borzacchini.

At Terni we were in twelfth place and finally at Perugia we were thirteenth at 96·8 km/h, always at the head of our class and with as much as 22 minutes' advantage on Lord Howe and Hamilton.

Our second supply depot was situated at Perugia, and there I gave over the wheel to Eyston after having driven continuously for 600 km of difficult roads. I had taken over the car in third place in our class and gave it back after having gained first place and with a lead of 22 minutes over the next competitor.

Eyston had sat beside me bravely for six hours as passenger, to the accompaniment of jerks and bumps, and was certainly not in the best physical condition when he took over the wheel. Soon after leaving Perugia we had to stop as he thought the frame was broken; however, he himself was later to confess in his memoirs that he had begun by then to 'imagine things' as our car, although it was no longer as fresh as when we started, was still in good condition. Our brakes had almost disappeared, and again we had to change a couple of sparking plugs, but altogether we were still going very strongly.

After Ancona we had to switch on the headlamps, and it was maddening to find that the dynamo had not been functioning properly and the battery was almost exhausted, so that the light from our enormous Lucas lamps was nothing like enough to let us take advantage of the speed of our car. The run through Pesaro, Rimini, Forli, and Faenza was even more frightening than usual! We arrived in a dense crowd at 160 km/h and the crowd opened up at the last moment leaving just a narrow lane through which we had to drive in the low beam of our lamps, hoping that we were not beheading some careless spectator leaning forward shouting encouragement!

We got to Bologna at about nine o'clock in the evening and to our third and last supply depot, situated just after the control at Porta Mazzini. We had taken 12 hours 56 minutes at an average of 93·7 km/h, and had passed nearly every car which had started before us. Our depot was in charge of McConnell, who had seen us off at Brescia and who from Bologna was going on to Brescia to meet us on our arrival. Birkin and Rubin, who had withdrawn from the race at Siena, were with him and they made a great fuss of us. The stop was a lengthy one, and Birkin very decently worked on the car too.

In addition to filling the MG with fuel, the mechanics tried to give new life to our brakes, adjust the shock-absorbers, and above all change the defective dynamo. However, it was not possible to dismount it so they tried instead to fit a new battery.

Sometimes it would seem as if inanimate objects become possessed of malignant spirits in order to create the most unthought-of obstructions! Certainly the spare battery, which was absolutely identical to the defective one just removed, would just not fit into the appropriate space, and the mechanics worked feverishly while precious minutes ticked away.

Suddenly we heard the roar of the motor of another car, and the other surviving MG with Lord Howe and Hamilton, whom we thought were many minutes behind us, arrived at the depot. All the advantage accumulated over 1200 km of road was cancelled. In fact now we only had the initial 2 minutes' advantage over Lord Howe, and we had not yet left the depot when he arrived!

The sight of the other MG was like a whiplash to us. In an instant the battery was installed somehow or other. George shot off like a bullet and I had to jump for it with the car on the move. The MG was going splendidly, but the electrics were far from well; only one of the lamps lit the road for Eyston who, however, was well into his stride on the fast roads of Veneto and was going very strongly, knowing that just behind us were Howe and Hamilton, who would not be sparing themselves.

Fortunately, my companion had trained very thoroughly on this stretch of road but, so far as I was concerned, it was a most unpleasant section, as the feeling of going along at full speed in the night with just a small beam of light to guide the driver is a terrifying experience; and Eyston was by now in fighting mood and would not give in.

By this time we had passed every vehicle which had left ahead of us and were with the very first car going through towns and villages. We were also ahead of our expected time of arrival, and so we often found the road blocked by vehicles and people, and our poor headlights certainly did not give the impression that it was one of the Mille Miglia cars arriving! So, in addition to all other troubles, we also had the thankless task of clearing the road.

It certainly was not a pleasant run, and when Eyston took one gutter at full speed I nearly flew out of the car and in saving myself gave my knee a most painful knock. I really thought, once or twice, that our race was going to end in a most drastic way! But Eyston was showing his real form and obviously knew what he was doing. At Treviso we still had 3 minutes' advantage on Lord Howe, but at Feltre our distance was reduced to only 3 seconds! I kept on looking back to see if I could distinguish in the distance the powerful headlamps of the other MG and nearing Vicenza I did in fact see the light of our pursuers!

At last we got to Verona where an enormous crowd filled the streets and the brilliantly lit restaurants. We were just on the point of taking the road to Brescia when the car became most unstable and finished up with an alarming swerve. A rear tyre was flat!

The MG had hardly stopped when I was out to change the wheel. Fortunately, we were still inside the town and the light of the street lamp helped me considerably. We looked feverishly for the jack — but no jack could we find. Originally, all the tools were placed near the mechanic's seat, but after all our stops to change eighteen plugs, and the lengthy halt at Bologna, my half of the car was a real 'old iron shop', where damaged sparking plugs, spanners, levers, banana peel, rags, and sandwiches covered in petrol were lying. But

the jack was not there. Fortunately, several of the locals came over and with a hearty heave the car was lifted, and I was able to change the wheel in an instant, and we were off again at full speed amidst shouts of 'Avanti' from our helpers.

I was still holding on grimly to the hammer when we came in sight of Brescia, and soon we shot up to the finishing line. We were the first to finish the Seventh Mille Miglia and everyone was already applauding us as the winners of our class; but I knew from a previous unfortunate experience how such applause can easily turn to bitter disillusion, and it still seemed probable to me that Howe and Hamilton could beat us. I therefore kept scrutinising the road and watching for the lights of the MG and, together with the timekeeper 'Bepi' Mazier, counted the passing seconds one by one.

Lord Howe had left 3 minutes after us and therefore all that mattered now was that self-same interval. I counted 1 minute, then 2, then 30–40 seconds, and no car in sight!... The last 20 seconds seemed never-ending. Then, at last, we were sure of our victory and we could relax and enjoy our triumph.

Barely 4 minutes after our arrival the headlights and far-away roar of an engine announced the approach of our friendly enemies. Soon Lord Howe and Hamilton were at the finish; but we had beaten them by just 90 seconds! It had been a terrific run and the margin at the finish was infinitesimal when one considers that we had been racing for 18 hours. Lord Howe's companion, Hamilton, had been driving very well from Bologna to the finish.

We could not understand how it was that in view of our puncture they had not overtaken us, but then we found out that they also had suffered a puncture just outside the town, and with traditional English phlegm had changed the wheel without the help of a human jack. This fact had enabled us to gain those precious seconds! The $1\frac{1}{2}$ minutes between us at the end was in fact due to the longer time they had taken to deal with their puncture.

Eyston and I won the 1100-cc class in 18 hours 1 minute 40 seconds at an average of 91·57 km/h, beating the previous record by 34 minutes. Lord Howe and Hamilton were second, 1 minute 30 seconds behind, and Ambrosini–Minchetti were third in a Fiat Siata, arriving 43 minutes later. We were twenty-first in the general classification. The Grand Prix of Brescia, the team prize, was won by MG and the winning of this gigantic trophy — a Roman chariot — almost larger than our small cars — set the seal on our victory.

3
Jack Brabham

MONACO GRAND PRIX 1959

After a racing career which spanned more than twenty years, and which came to a halt when my engine blew up in the 1970 Mexican Grand Prix, it is certainly not easy to single out one particular event as my greatest race. Indeed, thinking about it hard, I came to the conclusion that it was impossible to choose just one race, since there are several that stand out in my memory. Maybe they weren't all the best driving efforts, but some of them were great to me in that they marked a milestone in my progress — like the 1959 Monaco Grand Prix, which was my very first victory in a *grande épreuve*. Others were important to me because I felt I pulled off a good performance against the opposition, or overcame the prevailing conditions.

But I suppose that sunny day in Monte Carlo is something I shall never forget. Two years earlier, with a 2-litre version of the Coventry-Climax engine in a Cooper, I had come into contact rather rudely with a bit of the Principality (trying to get into the Casino via the back door!) during practice, but in the race I was running third to Fangio's Maserati and the Vanwall driven by Tony Brooks, when the fuel pump drive failed, and I had a punishing time pushing the car home to take sixth place. In 1958 there was a 2·2-litre Coventry-Climax engine for my Cooper, and this time I finished fourth (while Maurice Trintignant, in another Cooper, won the race).

By 1959 we had a Coventry-Climax engine up to the full permitted capacity of $2\frac{1}{2}$ litres, and with the extra power (plus added confidence from winning the Formula 1 race at Silverstone the week before), I went down to Monaco thinking that perhaps at last I would be able to pull off my first Grand Prix win.

There was, however, a question mark hanging over the race. At the end of the Silverstone race the water temperature gauge was right off the clock, and there was no time to discover what had caused this before the car was on its way down to the Mediterranean. There was a spare engine, but after a few practice laps round the Monaco circuit this, too, began to show signs of getting too hot. We weren't certain of Bruce McLaren's engine, either.

Fortunately, there was a magnificent team spirit in the Cooper set-up, and when he learned of my problems Masten Gregory came forward with a generous offer. Masten took John Cooper on one side the night before the race, told him he thought I had the better chance of doing well, and suggested his engine was fitted in my car.

This did not mean our worries were over though, for during practice we started to catch on

as to why the engines were overheating; it was due to faulty sealing rings between the engine block and the cylinder head, and with Bruce's engine also revealing signs of the same trouble it seemed likely that Masten's power unit might develop the same trouble during the stress of the race.

The weather was glorious that week at Monaco. (I remember an exhilarating drive up La Turbie in a Mercedes which the factory had sent for me to try, and being told sternly by Betty, my wife, to cut out the rallying approach!) In a way I wish it had been cooler, for we had another overheating problem in the Coopers; with the radiator in front and the pedals immediately behind, my feet quickly got roasted. We had run into the problem quite seriously during practice, and on the eve of the Grand Prix we spent a lot of time messing about with pieces of cardboard, trying to direct the hot air away from the cockpit. This made some difference, but in the race itself things got very uncomfortable indeed.

The front row of the grid consisted of Jean Behra, in a works Ferrari, Stirling Moss in Rob Walker's Cooper-Climax, and myself. At that time the start was on the harbour-side, and after we all got round the gasworks hairpin without shunting (rather to everyone's surprise!) the pattern settled down to Behra in the lead, Stirling trying all he knew to overtake him, and me hanging on a short distance behind.

At just over 20 laps, Stirling swooped past the Ferrari on the rise to the Casino; a few laps later I managed to squeeze by Behra to take second place. Then my gearbox started to play up, and I was finding it difficult to snatch first gear. This affected my lap times, and Stirling pulled away steadily to get an advantage of nearly half a minute, while I kept second place fairly comfortably from the Ferraris of Tony Brooks and Phil Hill.

14

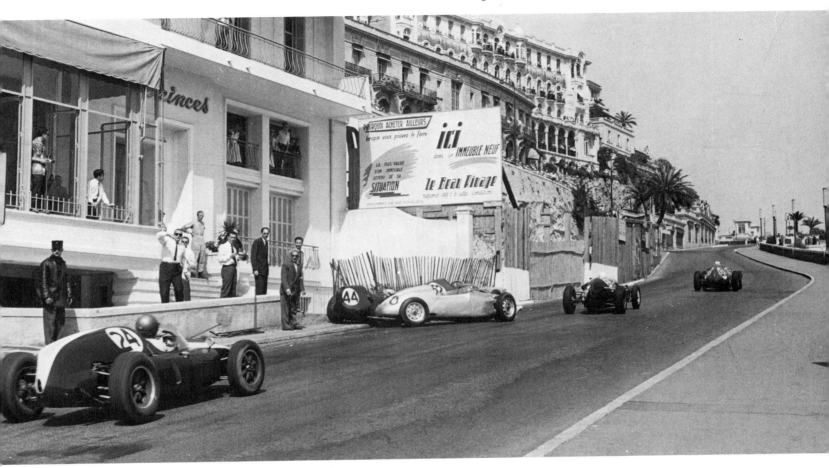

Jack Brabham (no. 24) challenging the leaders
during the 1959 Monaco Grand Prix.

Apart from the discomfort in the cockpit — my feet were starting to roast — I was still concerned about my engine, because I'd seen Masten Gregory pull in to retire after only a few laps, and I guessed it was the same old overheating problem.

Then suddenly Stirling's transmission failed. He was using a Colotti gearbox, which gave him a lot of trouble that season, and, fortunately for me, the Monaco race was one of those times when it went wrong. So I found myself in the lead, and facing another challenge. Signals from the Cooper pits informed me that Tony Brooks was putting on the pressure, so I had to give up any idea of saving my engine and concentrate on keeping ahead. My lap times improved, despite the oil and rubber which was thick around the circuit. I managed to go quicker than Stirling had gone earlier, and eventually set a new lap record before taking the chequered flag.

The heat on my feet became almost unbearable

15

before the finish, and I wondered whether I could last out before Tony Brooks caught me, but I gritted my teeth and thought longingly of a lovely cool bath!

It would be wrong to say I couldn't believe I had won my first world championship Grand Prix, but it was an emotional moment, and the crowds of spectators really terrified me. After I had hauled myself out of the cockpit and walked gingerly on my cooked feet to receive the trophy from Princess Grace, the enthusiastic fans swarmed around like bees. I remember one photographer, desperate to get a picture, stood on the bonnet of the Cooper and put a nasty dent in it. Despite my pleasure at winning I was furious that my great little car was being so shabbily treated, and just about blew my top. To make things worse, I still had a laurel wreath round my neck and the huge gold trophy under one arm. I had one hand free to sign autographs, and my writing certainly suffered.

It was some time before I could make my escape, but I had to beat the retreat in the Cooper, driving it some 5 miles back to my hotel along the coast.

In spite of the worries and sore feet, that Monaco Grand Prix stands out vividly in my memory. It gave me renewed confidence for the rest of the season, and set me on the road to my first world championship (which I clinched at Sebring, after running out of fuel on the last lap and pushing home the last 500 yards to finish fourth).

Naturally, the Monaco win gave me a soft spot for that fantastic round-the-houses circuit, but in fact I never won there again. Eleven years later, in what I knew was to be my last racing season, I thought I would achieve my ambition of repeating that 1959 victory . . . but lost it to Jochen Rindt on the last corner of the last lap when I slid into the straw bales and limped home into second place. If

I'd won the 1970 Monaco Grand Prix I reckon that would be one of my top races in a list of well over a hundred GPs but, as it was, I prefer to forget it!

For me, though, another outstanding day was in July 1966, when I drove my Repco-powered Brabham to victory in the French Grand Prix at Reims.

That year was the first season of the 3-litre formula, and the French round of the world championship was really the first time we had got the Repco engine and the chassis properly sorted and reliable. Though I had high hopes that the relatively simple Repco V8 would prove a race winner in the first year of the 3-litres, I hardly expected to run up a victory on such a fast circuit as Reims, which places a premium on brute power.

In practice I was clearly down on power compared with the V12 Ferraris, and had to settle for the second row of the grid, looking at the exhaust pipes of a brace of Ferraris driven by Lorenzo Bandini and Mike Parkes, and the Cooper-Maserati of John Surtees. Knowing that I was giving away something like 60 hp to the Ferraris, I was determined to keep with them if I could through slipstreaming.

Almost as soon as the race started Surtees ran into trouble, and this was a help since I was able to latch on to the Ferraris, squeeze past Mike Parkes round the back of the circuit, and retain the tow from Bandini. With the help of this tow we were able to pull away from the rest of the field. The big Ferrari gave me a tremendous pull down the very fast straights; down Thillois I was touching 182 mph with Bandini's assistance, but when I lost the tow after a dozen laps my maximum dropped to 174 mph.

It had been difficult keeping up with Bandini, though I was helped by my car handling better through the right and left curves before

Muizon. But it was too good to be true, and when we lapped a couple of slower machines I got bogged down in the 'traffic' and lost my slipstream assistance. After that there was nothing I could do to keep in contact with Bandini, though I found it possible to pull away fairly comfortably from Parkes.

Bandini had a lead of over half a minute at two-thirds distance, and there was nothing I could do about it, except hope that he might break down ... which he did. On lap 32 of this 48-lap race I saw the Ferrari pulled off at the side of the circuit at Thillois (his throttle cable had snapped) and knew that I was in the lead.

Later, I learned that the spectators started to get excited when Parkes began to catch me, but I wasn't really worried. I did a quick calculation in my head, compared the number of seconds he was cutting off my lead with the number of laps to go, and decided there was no need for a full-out effort.

So it all went well to the flag, and I won that French Grand Prix at an average of 136·9 mph, which made it at that time the second quickest championship GP ever held (beaten only by the 1959 German GP on the banked track).

If anything, I was more pleased about that victory than Monaco in 1959. It was the first win in a Grand Prix with an Australian engine, and the first win in a GP by a driver in a machine bearing his own name.

Looking back on it now, I suppose that that French GP win was by default. And I suppose you could say the same about victory in Monaco in 1959. All the same, you have to have your luck in motor racing, and you have to finish the course in order to be in with a chance of winning. Both of those two races meant a lot to me, because for different reasons they were each a breakthrough.

In fact, I had two far tougher races during the 1966 season, ones in which I had to call on everything of which I was capable. Winning those two Grands Prix — in Holland and Germany — is engraved in my memory for a different reason; they really had to be worked for and certainly weren't handed to me on a plate.

By the time we went to Zandvoort for the Dutch Grand Prix I had also won the British Grand Prix at Brands Hatch, with team-mate Denny Hulme second. Things were coming good, but motoring journalists had cottoned on to the fact that I had had my fortieth birthday in April, and were tagging me with the label the Old Man of Motor Racing. (They seemed to have forgotten that Fangio reached the pinnacle of his amazing career when in his forties.)

I'm a quiet sort of chap, but all this veteran talk began to get under my skin. So at Zandvoort I decided to prove that an 'old man' could win a Grand Prix. Just before the race began I put on a long false beard and limped up to the grid leaning on a jack handle. It caused something of a sensation, but as I did it I realised that after such a display I simply had to win the race. And as it turned out I had one of the hardest battles of my career.

When the flag fell I was fairly confident of seeing off the opposition, because our cars were really going beautifully, but I had not reckoned on a diabolically greasy track and the skill of Jim Clark. Someone dropped a load of oil on the circuit, which meant that I lost my power advantage over Jimmy, whose Lotus had only a 2-litre Climax. I had to work very gingerly with the throttle, and it was extremely difficult to get the power on to the road.

Things got to such a desperate state that I decided it would be better to follow Jimmy rather than try to head him and perhaps go off the road. I calculated that the condition of the circuit would

Brabham cornering at Monaco in his Cooper.

probably improve, and determined to have a real go at Jimmy in the closing laps.

Unfortunately, it didn't work out to plan, because even more oil was being dropped; it must have been coming from more than one car, because of the amount. So I had to change my plan, grit my teeth and set about driving really seriously. My pits told me I was beginning to cut back Jimmy's lead, which at one stage was 10 seconds. Jimmy got the message, too, and drove even harder to hold me at bay, but I managed to overhaul him gradually. Towards the end of the race the Lotus started to run into trouble, eventually finishing third after a couple of pit stops, but I think I could have caught Jimmy anyway. It gave me a shock, though, and I didn't play any more pranks before a Grand Prix!

The next Grand Prix wasn't easy, either. Indeed, that thrash round the Nurburgring, which gave me four GP victories in succession, was probably one of the most concentrated efforts I made in any race. The Grand Prix was run in quite shocking conditions because of heavy rain, making this most daunting of circuits terribly treacherous. Not only that, but conditions changed from lap to lap; sometimes I'd find a river running across the road when I came round a corner, and the next time it had shifted to a different point.

Those were 15 laps I shall always remember. I had to get stuck in right from the start, because I failed to make the front row of the grid through gearbox trouble in practice, and in conditions like that the only place to be is in front of everyone else. It wasn't until near the end of the first lap that I managed to get the jump on John Surtees, who was driving a Cooper-Maserati, and after I got by he kept up the pressure, clearly hoping that I would be forced into error.

It was a tense time, and I could never relax my concentration for a single moment, knowing that John Surtees was only too ready to take advantage if I did. In fact, it was John who slipped when he had a spin on lap 6, but he recovered wonderfully, reduced a 5 seconds' gap to only 2 seconds by the end of lap 7, and then dogged me relentlessly. It wasn't until lap 13 that I managed to get off the hook, when John started having clutch trouble.

When it was all over, and I got out of my car to go to the winner's rostrum, I was not only wet but as limp as a rag. In terms of my own personal driving effort this was probably my greatest race.

4
Philippe Etancelin

FRENCH

GRAND

PRIX

1930

One of my fondest motor-racing memories is of a competition I had decided I would not enter. In fact if it had not been for my wife I would now be denied the exciting recollections of the drama which preceded the French Grand Prix at Pau in 1930.

I raced as an independent for twenty-seven years. It was not the easy way to success, as anyone who has tried it will understand. Spares, transport, and mechanics — all these essential matters in what today would be called the logistics of motor-racing — are the concern of the independent driver. He cannot avoid responsibilities like a driver in a works team. Notwithstanding my independent status, however, I had had more than my fair share of success in 1930. It

20

was a tremendous sporting year in which I won the Morocco 100 Kilometres from Casablanca to Magazan; the race on the Frejus circuit in France; the Grand Prix from Le Dauphine to Grenoble; the Grand Prix Centenaire in Algeria; the Eight Hours Race in Algiers, and the eliminations for the Italian Grand Prix at Monza. Yet I decided that I would not race in the Grand Prix at Pau which was run in those days on the Toulouse road.

My confidence after the victories was not enough to overcome my doubts about my ability to do well in a prestigious international event which was sure to attract the greatest racing drivers of the day. The official teams of the British, Italians, and French would all be so powerful that I would have no chance. I decided not to submit my application form. And the more I thought about it, the more I was convinced I had made the right decision. I had had a good season and it would be a pity to mar it by entering a race in which the odds were so heavily against me. Besides I really wanted, after so many absences, to return to Rouen to look after my business. It was nothing to do with engineering. If it had been I daresay racing as an independent would have been just a little easier. In fact my commercial activities were concerned with selling wools for mattresses and, more especially, exporting the feathers and down of geese and ducks for pillows, bolsters, and eider-downs!

And while I was busily convincing myself of my wisdom in standing down from the race, my wife had sent my entry form to the French Automobile Club. Her point of view was the exact opposite of my own humble arguments. At Pau I would be racing against rivals of similar skill. To lower my sights at this stage would be foolish.

We talked it over at length and eventually I decided without any enthusiasm to go to the line-up at Pau. The competition was indeed fierce. There were 14 other Bugattis in the race besides my own, and furthermore the official Bugatti works team had no fewer than three drivers and a reserve all racing in cars more powerful than mine. The team Bugattis were 2·3 litres supercharged, whereas mine was 2 litres supercharged.

Feeling at a distinct disadvantage during the trials I was over-keen to show them my paces. A devil got into me and I drove unwisely and, of course, broke everything: shafts, pistons, block. All these vital spares were needed and the week-end was only a few hours away. My decision to stay out of this race seemed to have been vindicated — rather late! — and I decided to pack up the useless car and return to Rouen. I shrugged with indifference when my wife and my mechanic, Marius, stepped in again, urging me to waste no time in telephoning the Bugatti works. I did so and it was lucky for me that Marco, Bugatti's racing chief, was there and very unwilling to help me! I took it as a challenge that an old friend like Marco should refuse me. I could see him shaking his head as he told me, quite rightly; 'My firm is racing, Philippe. I cannot send spares to an unofficial competitor!' We argued for a long time and I pleaded so hard that eventually he gave in and with his usual kindness promised to put everything I needed on the very next plane to Biarritz.

On Saturday evening, well before the plane's arrival time, I was standing on the tarmac of Biarritz aerodrome with a thumping heart. I need not have worried. As I took possession of the

cases I saw that Marco had been as good as his word. Everything I needed was there. I departed for Pau as soon as possible and left the mechanics working through the night, preparing my Bugatti for Sunday's race. While they worked, I slept until five o'clock in the morning when Marius awakened me, telling me he wanted me to drive the Bugatti for about 100 km to run in the engine. Despite everyone's faith and devotion, even their tired enthusiasm at that early hour of the day, I was still discouraged to be entering an important race in these conditions.

I felt little better at the start of the race. My misfortunes during trials had persuaded me to choose a big rear axle couple which I felt would probably ensure an honourable place rather than a resounding victory and would at the very least lower the risk of my car breaking up again.

At last, still far from happy, I set off with the other 23 competitors on the first lap of the race. It was significant that after only 100 metres Lehoux broke his gearbox, returning to his pit on foot, choking with rage and, so I was told, quite unable to utter a word. No doubt his mechanic was relieved! But every race has its casualties and the Grand Prix at Pau in 1930 must still be sticking in the minds of several unlucky drivers whose cars came to the starting grid imperfectly prepared. For example, some time after Lehoux's departure I noticed trouble brewing — almost literally — in the cars of the official Bugatti team. They had all put on too small a rear axle couple with 15 teeth and in the course of the race I thrice saw a driver with a red scarf, the identification of the official Bugatti drivers, slowing down because of the character-istic smoke pouring from the tail end of his car.

In the earlier stages of the race I had stayed behind the Bugatti team. There were in fact 15 Bugattis among the 23 starters, but the works team was, I felt, my only real threat. When their axle trouble had banished them to their pits, I found myself in the lead. And after that I had only to nurse my car and keep my eye on the pits where my wife – as she did throughout the whole of my international motor-racing career – was giving the signals which told me where I stood in the race. The only possible threat to me was H. R. S. Birkin in his 4½-litre Bentley. I knew that his supercharged car was much faster than mine on the straight but that I could maintain a higher average speed because mine was considerably faster on the bends. Nevertheless he put up a tremendous fight to come in second, finishing only a little over 3 minutes behind me.

I was the first independent driver to win the Grand Prix of the French Automobile Club. Winning pleased me, of course. But I had been so dogged by doubt during the preliminaries that the victory itself is less important to me than the incidental dramas and discoveries, the misfortunes, and the lessons which remain in my mind. Nothing went smoothly for me on that September day in 1930. Hence the race itself was only dimly in my mind until a few years ago when I went back to the Pau circuit. I was astounded to see again the very narrow road, lined with trees, and to remember that during the race we averaged nearly 100 mph. It was pleasant to look back on an event which seemed to have happened in another age.

My wife and I reminisced about the 1930 Grand Prix and soon we were recalling the incidents and experiments. For instance I used a fuel, elcosine, which was new to France but had been used in Italy. I had insisted on reliable Terlor plugs. It was details like these which had, I decided, gained me 3 and 4 seconds a lap. I recalled also that on the Thursday before the race I had carried out some consumption tests. According to these my Bugatti should have had 15 litres of petrol still in the tank by the time I passed the chequered flag. And I remember now that we checked the tank on the following Monday to find that it contained a mere wine-glass full. We were, to say the least, shocked. Another surprise awaited us when we carried out a detailed overhaul of the car later. The clutch was held in position by only two of the original six nuts. It would seem that I got home only just in time.

But I did win. Official congratulations followed. I even gave my impressions over the radio. It was the very beginning of news broadcasting in France and I still smile to recall the rickety ladder I had to climb to reach the broadcasting studio. Only a fortnight after Pau I was at San Sebastian preparing for the start of the Spanish Grand Prix when His Majesty King Alphonso XIII did me the honour of congratulating me, on a race I never wished to compete in! That was, I suppose, one of the greatest moments of my sporting career.

The 24 Hours Race in Le Mans in 1934 is connected with the Grand Prix of the French Automobile Club in 1930 because these were the two high spots of my career as an independent racing driver.

In 1934 I had a gentleman's agreement with M. Tinaly, Director-General of Eco-Standard, for the races that season, and at the beginning of the year he had asked me to enter for the Le Mans 24 Hours Grand Prix d'Endurance. My reply was prompt and to the point. I told him that I preferred to race in the Formula 1 speed Grands Prix because I had never attempted the Le Mans and considered myself qualified only for the 300–600 km contests. He would not listen to my objections and finally persuaded me to enter for Le Mans – against my better judgment.

Accordingly I left with my wife for Milan to collect my new supercharged Alfa Romeo 2·3-litre car for the race. At the factory I particularly asked that it should be handed over to me at least two months before the race so that I could do the

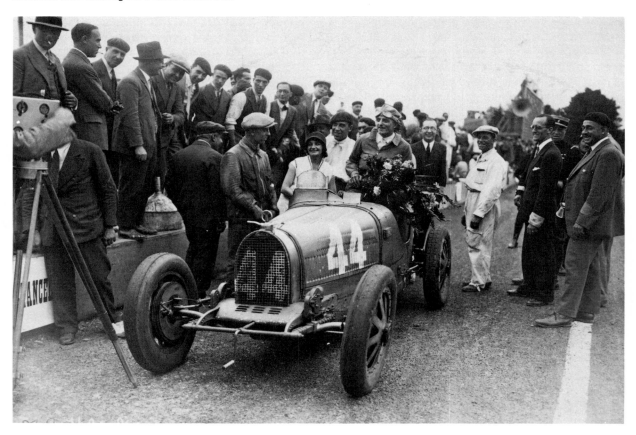

final tuning myself. I wanted also to adapt myself to the machine which was designed for Le Mans. The promises they made in Milan were not kept and I was acutely disappointed that it did not arrive at Le Mans until a mere two hours before the weigh-in closed. The result of this was that I was able to drive only a few laps with my co-driver, Luigi Chinetti, and this brief acquaintance with the car was not enough to prevent some difficulties which arose during the race.

To begin with I let Chinetti take the wheel as I was not used to the Le Mans start and feared that

I might lose valuable time if, by force of habit, I forgot myself and imagined I was at the start of a Grand Prix speed race. During the first hours before our initial refuelling, Chinetti was 2 or 3 laps behind so that when I took over, my nerves were tense – in spite of Chinetti's repeated calm recommendations that I get it into my head we were there for 24 hours! I was unable to follow his advice – completely incapable of conquering my passion for speed. So, to make up for the hours I had sat impatiently beside him as he drove, I took the wheel grimly in my hands and trod on the accelerator pedal as if I was competing in a speed race.

Not unnaturally this enabled me to beat the lap record; but in doing so I threw the Alfa seriously out of joint. After stopping at our pit for the second refuelling, the lamps and shock absorbers were badly shaken and at each stop thereafter we had to tighten up what I had shaken loose with my reckless speeding. Having got every last ounce of power out of the car — more, by far, than she should have given — the petrol tank developed a slight leak. This was caused by the spare wheel rubbing the tank. So to avoid leakage, we mobilised everyone at the pit to chew as much gum as they could to block the leak. Friends and spectators, calling at our pit for news, were pressed into service and asked to give up their gum when we made a pit stop.

Having driven at a hellish pace trying to keep up with me, most of our serious rivals had ended by damaging their machines, so that around three o'clock in the morning we were leading comfortably by 8 or 9 laps. From then on I felt we could breathe more easily — and, more to the point, nurse the Alfa to the end of the race.

At the finish there had to be drama, of course. On the 58th minute of the 23rd hour when Chinetti was at the wheel, he slowed down to hand over to me so that I, as the owner, could take the Alfa over the finishing line and enjoy the plaudits of the crowd. My reply to his gesture was quite simply to order him to carry on. I was not impatient or ill-humoured. I merely wished to pay homage to his courage and skill, giving him the satisfaction of stopping on the winner's line. As it happened it was a far happier inspiration than I had imagined for when we should have driven the final lap of honour, it was quite impossible to get the car to start. If we had stopped for Chinetti to hand over the wheel to me, we would have been the last and most conspicuous casualty of the event — and lost the 1934 Le Mans.

We decided to leave the injured Alfa to enjoy her rest while we went off to celebrate. Tinaly was, of course, overjoyed at the result of the test and vowed to exhibit the Alfa — 'Winner of the 1934 Le Mans 24 Hours' in one of those prestigious Champs Elysées windows. He hardly seemed to realise how near he came to having an empty window.

5
Mario Andretti

INDIANAPOLIS
500
1969

The evening after the 1968 Indianapolis 500 Mile race, I humbly accepted my cheque for the thirty-third — and final — position. I knew that people were saying that here was another upstart tottering on the brink of being defeated by Indy. I had won two national driving championships and set speed records on every paved mile track in the United States Auto Club competition. But Indy — oh, Indy. How that place had hurt me!

Twice I had been favoured to win and had dropped out early with mechanical difficulties. This time I sat at the far end of the speakers' table — the biggest loser of all. Ignominious? That's only half of it. When my machine quit after only 2 laps, I jumped into another. The second car gave up after 24 laps. Thus, I was also the co-owner of twenty-seventh place. That night, I vowed that some day, somehow, I was going to win my duel with Indy.

In the winter of 1968 I thought I had found the method. I heard that Colin Chapman was preparing a radically new Lotus with four-wheel drive for the 1969 500 Mile race. Chapman builds cars that win. He revolutionised racing at Indianapolis when he came over with the immortal Jimmy Clark and the Lotus in 1963.

At that time, many Americans wanted no part of the cars, claiming that Chapman operated on a very thin safety margin in his efforts to make his cars as light as possible. However, I was intrigued by the cars and impressed by the fact that he usually seemed to be coming up with something better while competitors were copying his old models.

Chapman, naturally, wasn't very taken with the idea of turning over a new car — a model that he thought would be his best ever — to anybody outside Team Lotus. However, after much trans-Atlantic conversation, some gentle persuasion, and use of a bit of leverage, Colin agreed to sell me a Lotus!

We tested the car at Hanford, California, early in 1969 and, to our great dismay, it was a real mess. It ran about 4 seconds slower than my old car, the front end was flying, the steering was bad, and the springs and brakes worse. It was just flat out spooky. We put together a list of 85 items which we wanted changed, and I came up with 10 more on the homeward-bound plane.

However, Colin was not dismayed. He thanked us and went back to work. The car was waiting when our crew arrived in Indianapolis on 1 May 1969. Chapman had made the suggested changes and had added a few wrinkles of his own. It was a gorgeous machine.

Suddenly, the anxiety and frustrations that hovered like a cloud of gloom over our garage in 1968 were gone. This baby looked like a winner. On 5 May I gave the Lotus a shakedown run and I really was impressed. I hit a 160·5 mph cruising speed on a few laps.

Right then we decided to take our time and bring it as close to perfect trim as humans can achieve with a race car. Our practices became routine. I would run a few laps, then we would push it back to the garage for minor adjustments. Slowly, almost without any extra effort on my part, the speed of the Lotus crept upward.

On the Wednesday before the scheduled opening of qualifications, I turned a lap at 171·657 mph, just a tick under Joe Leonard's one-lap record of 171·953. I was seeing nothing but rainbows. People thought I was extending the 'needle' but I meant it when I said I had not yet fully extended the car. I was thinking big numbers. Like a 174 mph average for the four qualifying laps, with, perhaps, a top lap in the 175 range.

Rain wiped out the first week-end of qualifications and caused our strategy to flip-flop. We had planned to qualify on the first day, then take nearly two weeks to work on a problem that had been nagging the cars that were powered by turbo-Fords.

The engines were running well, but they were gobbling fuel at an alarming rate. We had been averaging about 1·4 miles per gallon. The car starts the race with 72 gallons in the tank and the rules allow only an additional 250 gallons in the pit. Some fuel will get sloshed around during a pit stop, and there is a possibility that, because the gravity feed is lessened, the crew will be unable to get all of the fuel out of the pit tank once the tank is low. Chances were good that a man averaging 1·4 miles per gallon would be looking for a horse before the 200th lap.

Since time was no longer our ally, we began

practising immediately, with a full load of fuel, but late Monday afternoon we hit a snag. A right rear universal joint broke. When the U-joint snapped, I over-revved the engine and it blew. The weakness of the U-joints was one of the things that we had noted during our testing at Hanford, and Chapman already had some stronger ones that he planned to install for the race.

The crew needed all of Tuesday to repair the car and to install new U-joints. Since considerable work had been done on the right side, Jimmy McGee, co-chief mechanic of the crew, with Clint Brawner, had all of the running gear (hubs and everything) on that side of the car magnafluxed. He wanted to be certain that nothing had been overlooked.

We practised Wednesday morning and everything seemed to be in good shape. Wednesday afternoon, about three-forty, we decided to try a high-speed run. I took two slow laps, then moved to the middle of the track as I came down the main straightaway. When I am preparing to run my first hot lap of a practice session, I follow a standard procedure. I stand on it down the back stretch, feel my way through turn No 3, then really cut loose in the short chute in order to get a good run out of No 4 turn. Going down the back stretch and through turn No 3, everything sounded lovely.

I never got out of No 4. Just as I pointed the car into the fourth turn, I heard a 'whirr-r-r'. It's a sickening sound to a race driver. It means something is coming off the machine.

At first I thought another U-joint had broken and torn the suspension. But, as the car spun around, I saw a wheel in the air. The right rear of the car dug in and slammed me backwards into the wall. All sorts of garbage started flying off the car. The hood popped off and slammed into the wall, causing observers down the track to believe that the car was upside down.

The moment the car hit the wall, I felt intense heat — fire! I thank the Dear Lord that I wasn't stunned by the impact. I covered my face with one hand and unsnapped the seat-belt with the other. By this time I could feel the heat through my uniform. That wasn't too bad, but the heat around my face was almost unbearable.

I managed to jump out while the car was still moving. Art Pollard, who had been right behind me in an STP team car and did a beautiful job of steering through my mess without crashing, ran over to help me.

Right away, I asked Pollard, 'What about my face?' His answer was a great relief: 'It's starting to blister, so that's a good sign. I would say first degree — second in some places at the worst.' Fear of burns is something that haunts all race drivers, and I had been afraid that they were much worse. A trip to the field hospital inside the track confirmed that the burns were minor — if extremely painful.

I returned to a gloomy garage. Here we were, three days before qualifications and my once-beautiful race car was a hunk of burned and twisted metal. There were two questions I wanted answered immediately: First, what caused the accident? and second, how long would it take to prepare another car? Jimmy already had discovered that a hub had sheared off, causing the car to lose its right rear wheel. There obviously had been an imperfection in the metal. An investigation showed that there had been a crack in the hub. That meant one thing to me: somebody hadn't done his job when the parts were magnafluxed that morning. That hub never should have been passed, and the oversight had nearly cost me my life.

Andy Granatelli, our car owner, and Chapman had spare cars, but they were a good four days away from top shape. Colin offered us Jochen

Rindt's car and we mulled that over for a few minutes. While I don't think it was a conscious thing, I was inclined to pass. After all, I had just been bitten by a Lotus. We decided that the only route was to go for broke with our spare car — a Brawner-McGee Hawk that we had run in two earlier races.

The crew worked all night and we were back on the track the following day. We weren't just out there, we were competitive. I turned a lap at 168·602. There was no time for refinements; we had to approach every situation with an 'I'll-think-about-it-tomorrow' attitude. The pole position looked like a lost cause, but I was determined to qualify up front.

A. J. Foyt, a three-times winner, secured the pole with speed of 170·558 mph. I surprised many — including, maybe, myself — by landing beside him in the middle of the front row with a 169·851 average. Bobby Unser, the defending champion, took the outside position.

The qualifying ordeal over, we discovered that once again we were tottering on the edge of a deep pit. We had been plagued by heating problems, far from small ones. But, with little time to get ready after the accident, we had decided to take first things first.

We knew that the car would need an extra radiator belt in order to run safely at high speeds during the race. Without one, there was danger that the car would overheat faster than a two-dollar pistol.

There is a rule that, once a car has qualified, nothing can be added that will change the body configuration. We didn't need the extra radiator for qualifying, but we wanted to be legal. Brawner asked three members of the Technical Committee if they thought the additional radiator would change the body configuration. If so, he added, we would put on a dummy for qualifications.

They told him the dummy wouldn't be necessary.

The day after we qualified, the crew hung the thing behind the cockpit and it was as if we had robbed the American Express. Crew chiefs let out yelps that could be heard in Detroit. This set off a series of arguments that lasted into the night. However, the next morning, Chief Steward Harlan Fengler announced that cars would not be allowed to race with radiators or coolers that were not attached when they qualified.

The ruling hit us like a bomb. We honestly believed that we would not be able to go 200 laps without the additional radiator. Sick isn't the proper word for the way I felt. It seemed at the moment that curing leprosy would be a parlour trick compared with the task I was facing. And I thought, 'This was going to be a great month, but it looks like all I will have to show for it will be a face full of blisters.' However, we were there to race and I was going to try to get the most out of what I had.

I slipped past Foyt and took the lead in the first turn at the start of the race. I had no intention of pouring on the coal and trying to stay out in front as long as I could. First, I didn't have that much confidence in the engine's durability, and second, I believed my only chance was to subject the car to stress at the beginning, find the problems, sort them out, and plan a race that would keep me running within the car's limitations and still remain competitive.

Just as we guessed, the gauges immediately headed for the sky. The oil pressure hit 270, the water 240. Normally, 220 would be about right for the oil and 190–200 for the water. I played around a little with the power and found that if I dropped down a couple of hundred revs I moved right into the ball park — 225 on the water, 240 on the oil. The overheating situation was nowhere near as serious as we had feared.

Andretti (no. 2) leading Ruby during the 1969 Indianapolis 500.

On the fifth lap, I got my first good fright of the long day when I felt a spray in the cockpit. Since the gauges were flickering between dangerous and 'give up' at the time, I thought, 'That's it, Buster. You've had it again.' I had no doubt that the radiator had sprung a leak. I slowed my speed and Foyt moved around me to take the lead.

It took a few seconds, but I located the source and heaved a huge sigh of relief. The crew had strapped a bottle of liquid (from which I was to quench my thirst from time to time during the race) behind the cockpit. A rubber hose had been run out of the cap and strapped to the shoulder of my uniform. You get a certain amount of air current in the cockpit, and it had tipped the bottle.

Roger McCluskey, Foyt's team-mate, also slipped past me while I was solving the puzzle, so I fell in behind McCluskey and tried to stay close, catch a draught from his car and conserve precious fuel. The three of us ran pretty much like we were on a string for 40 laps but, by this time, the party had grown. Wally Dallenbach and Lloyd

30

Ruby had charged from the seventh row and were applying plenty of pressure from our immediate rear.

Then McCluskey got a foul break. He ran out of fuel. By the time he coasted into the pits and got out again, he had lost 15 positions. Foyt and I both pitted on the 51st lap. My crew had planned slow pit stops, hoping that by taking our time we would lose a minimum of fuel while refilling the tanks. What we didn't plan was a little trip to the squirrel farm I attempted on the way out of the pits.

The driver is always in a hurry to get out of the pits but he must be careful not to over-rev the engine and slip the clutch; but the confounded critter got away from me. Quickly, I leaned on the power and got out and I'll be the first to admit that it was mostly luck. I'd say that nine times out of ten, a clutch would have turned to putty on the spot.

Foyt got out 15 seconds ahead of me. On top of that, I had to take it easy for a while and allow my clutch to cool. While I was doing penance for my sins, Ruby roared around me into second place.

After a few laps, I gingerly tested the clutch. Yep, it was still there. And for the first time it occurred to me that maybe — just maybe — this was going to be my day. After a few more laps my pit signals began revealing a very interesting message. Ruby, just a few car lengths in front of me, and I, were gaining on Foyt at the rate of nearly 2 seconds a lap.

All of a sudden we came out of a turn and there he was — right in our sights. We both rolled around him on the 79th lap. Foyt pitted with a major ailment — the turbocharger wasn't working. He stayed in the pits 24 minutes, finally coming back to finish eighth.

The longer I went, the better the car seemed to run, and I soon moved around Ruby and regained the lead. Ruby is a tough competitor and he was a real tiger that afternoon; but I felt confident that I could hold him off — if the strain didn't bring back all of my engine ailments.

Along came lap 104, another pit stop, another trauma. Indy cars have two fuel tanks. Fuel is fed into them simultaneously by two hoses. For some unaccountable reason, the hose on the far side wasn't feeding properly. Jimmy cleared his, then we sat and waited for Clint. And waited. And waited. And waited. The official chart says I was in the pit some 40 seconds. It is wrong. I was in at least a day and a half!

Ruby, now leading, had gained so much time he could make a pit stop and retain the lead. Lloyd pitted on the 106th lap — and was dealt a haymaker by the horrible hand of fate. Lloyd tried to return to action before one of the hoses was disengaged. The pressure ripped off the fuel tank fittings and flooded his pit. He was out of the race.

This unexpected turn of events left the man who sneaked out of town under cover of darkness in 1968 after finishing thirty-third! Nobody else was even close. By the 110th lap I had a margin of more than a lap on the survivors. My only worries now were the engine and fuel, but the sudden lack of competition allowed me to relax the pressure on the equipment.

As it turned out, there was only one major problem — me. I did all I could to turn a routine finish into a Chinese fire-drill. On the 150th lap, Mike Mosley was minding his own business going into the No 2 turn. Here came Momma Andretti's little race driver creeping up behind him and thinking about everything except what he was doing.

I got caught in his draught and the next thing I knew, I was sideways and drifting towards the wall. And I mean way up there. I was well into the grey stuff before I finally got the car under control.

On the 153rd lap, I made my third and final pit

stop. Same old thing. Time to read a book. But leave it to me to add excitement in a dull situation. I pulled away before Clint was ready and I hit him with the car, giving him a nasty bump on the leg!

Friends told me later that Clint never even quit smiling. He had waited nineteen years for this moment. They would have had to kill him to get him out of those pits. All he kept doing was patting that big tank and smiling more. There was still fuel in it.

The final 57 laps were merely an exercise in concentration. I had an overwhelming urge to nurse the car around the track, but when I tried that, I got out of my pattern, backing off too early and wiggling dangerously in those turns. Once I just clean forgot what I was doing and flirted with the concrete again.

Jimmy's face was a mask as he calmly gave me pit signals every time around. Clint, looking for his first Indy triumph, was pacing our little pit. Granatelli, who had come so close before without tasting victory, sat like a great stone Buddha in the pits — refusing to accept congratulations or even to speak.

I could see the people in the great crowd on their feet, waving scorecards and handkerchiefs — waving me on. Starter Pat Vidan dropped the white flag. One lap to go. One trip around a $2\frac{1}{2}$-mile race-track. One very long journey from a displaced persons camp in Italy to the top of the world.

The record book shows that I led for 116 of the 200 laps, established 15 records during the race, including a new 500-mile standard of 156·867 mph and collected a purse of $205,727.06. The record book does not recount what is most important to me. I had climbed the mountain. I had conquered Indy.

6

Piero Taruffi

MILLE MIGLIA
1957

My career, on two wheels and four, began in 1923. It spanned three and a half decades before my retirement in 1957. My 'greatest race' was my last — the 1957 Mille Miglia.

I approached that race in a troubled state of mind, considering whether the time had arrived for me to retire. I had just come second to Gendebien in the Tour of Sicily. Although placed first in my class (with a Maserati 3000 six-cylinder sports model) I was very conscious of the fact that it was the third time I had missed winning the famous Sicilian event. And I had damaged the Maserati 95 miles from the finishing post in circumstances which troubled me.

I have often wondered about that mistake. Why did I go wrong on that corner? Up to that point I

33

had been perfectly in charge. Was it inattention due to fatigue or was there something treacherous about the road surface that I had not noticed? It is a doubt which I have never been able to settle. One other mistake I certainly made: I should have inspected the damage before continuing to drive. The bracket supporting the steering box was broken and it was obviously crazy to have gone on. A driver of my age and experience could hardly be blinded by the excitement of the race. Was I still 'young' and over-enthusiastic, or was I simply reckless? These questions tipped the scale when I came to consider retiring.

My second place in the Sicilian race was not appreciated by Ugolini (the Maserati Team Manager). I realised this when the question of signing me up for the Mille Miglia arose. For my part, too, I remembered the hasty way the Maseratis had been prepared the year before; they came out from the coachbuilders practically on the eve of the race, with no time for a thorough test. My crash was partly due to this. There is nothing impromptu about the Mille Miglia; it requires serious preparation of both man and machine.

Enzo Ferrari, who had always shown great confidence in me where this tough race was concerned, now got in touch, saying that he would willingly place a car at my disposal. I went to see him and our interview was most cordial. His attitude was more paternal than ever before — he went so far as to advise me to give up racing after this Mille Miglia, which he was quite sure I would win. Of course, I knew that he held out the same certainty of victory to all his drivers; all the same, I was grateful for his confidence, and went home determined to do everything possible to bring victory to the House of Maranello. I saw quite a lot of him before the race, as the cars were based at his fine modern factory at Maranello, near Modena,

and it was there the cars were prepared and we set out for practice. He was always about, because Ferrari is a man who is entirely dedicated to his work. He lives for that factory of his. He seldom leaves Modena, even to see his cars race, except for the last few Mille Miglias, when he went to the refuelling depots at Ravenna and Bologna. Ferrari must be the only manufacturer in racing who has never seen one of his machines receive the chequered flag — as he could well have done many, many times!

During the Modena stay my wife was always by my side. When I took a car out on test she would sit in the yard in front of the works, reading or knitting in our car, and perhaps praying that Ferrari's prophecy and her husband's dream would come true. She knew how much I longed to win the Mille Miglia and how, for one reason and another, I thought I never should — so much so that I had promised her that the day I won it I would give up racing. One evening when I returned from a test run my wife, Ferrari, and I were all in this courtyard. He listened to my impressions and passed on instructions to the mechanics, while my wife longed only to get back to our hotel. Ferrari suggested that I should do at least one whole lap of the circuit in the actual race car, doing the northern half one day and the southern part the next. I said I would take a mechanic on the first stretch; and if the trials were satisfactory I should very much like my wife as passenger on the second day. Ferrari agreed. The car was prepared exactly as it would be on race day, with full tank and the tyre pressures recommended by the manufacturers. My seat was precisely tailored to fit, and I had had foam rubber stuck on the left-hand side of the cockpit so that the jolting would not injure the delicate scar tissue of my leg, a legacy from a Tripoli crash. We had also fitted a small and adjustable auxiliary windscreen, which

Taruffi at the start of the 1957 Mille Miglia.

could be raised above the ordinary one to protect me when following close behind other cars. I had also fitted numerous compartments in the driver's door: one for spare goggles, one for detergent and chamois leather to clean them with, and finally one for thirst-quenching sweets. Ferraris had done everything I asked, to the smallest detail.

My wife was much impressed with the car's acceleration. In second it could spin its wheels even at 90–95 mph, and one's body was pressed back into the seat with a force not far short of its own weight. The cars we passed seemed to be standing still, and whenever there was 200 or 300 yards of clear road the speed went straight over 125 mph. Naturally we never touched the car's maximum, which was 175 mph; I deduced this figure without taking chances, by timing the car at half the max revs attained during timed runs on a straight stretch of the Via Emilia (with 2 miles to get up speed), on the Formigine straight at Maranello. Isabella was thrilled. Her only complaint was the excessive heat from the engine. At one point I saw out of the corner of my eye that she had hung her feet out in the breeze – an effective means of air cooling! A timely storm near Viterbo reduced the temperature somewhat, and she was surprised to find that although this was an open car her helmet and goggles got only slightly wet, the rest of her kept quite dry. But she changed her views suddenly when we had to stop for a level-crossing.

At Siena we met von Trips, who was practising too, as he was refuelling his Ferrari and we ran in company towards Florence. Beyond Florence comes the fast but twisty Mugello stretch, past little towns almost hidden behind their screen of cypress trees. We admired the castle of the Medici, left the Gerini estates on one side and then began climbing up towards the Futa and Raticosa passes. I played leader and von Trips

followed close behind. There was not much traffic and the road simply invited high speeds. I accepted the invitation, and really started motoring, partly to see what the German was made of, for he was going to be one of our toughest opponents. When we got to Gualtieri's restaurant, which is half a mile from the beginning of the Raticosa, I stopped. It was a nice little place much frequented by people from Bologna because of its good cooking, and my wife and I knew it well, having often slept there on our way from Rome to Milan. The bed was huge and very high, and they still used an old-fashioned brass warming-pan. In winter when it was snowing we liked to eat in the big kitchen, with its copper pans and huge fireplace, while our hostess cooked delicious veal cutlets *alla fiorentina*. I had hardly ordered a table for three when von Trips arrived, saying that he had had trouble with the gear-change and would like me to try it. I too found that second was hard to engage. After a light meal we pressed on through Modena to Maranello, where we found Ferrari awaiting us, along with the rest of the team, Collins, de Portago, and Gendebien, who had likewise been practising.

The race was now only two days away. Early next morning the cars were driven over to Modena, where they and their drivers were immortalised by numerous photographers in the car-park at Ferrari headquarters. I remember that sunny morning very well. Peter Collins, in his funny little coloured woollen hat, kept nattering eagerly with his young wife, Louise, while von Trips, looking restless and slightly on edge, peered into one car after another, perhaps trying to spot points of difference. De Portago, looking like a rather unkempt grandee with his thick black hair, had on his favourite old black suede jacket and was taking cine films as usual.

How familiar it all was by now! Each Mille

Miglia the same. I thought back to 1931, when Ferrari was still racing the Alfa team, and I set out for Brescia from this very yard with Lelio Pellegrini; the next year it was Eugenio Siena. One by one I went through in my mind the races in which I had driven cars from the prancing horse stables: '49, '52, and '55. Looking around at my young team-mates I felt almost out of it; they were so exactly as I had been, filled with the same enthusiasm, the same terrific desire to succeed. And while they, in the prime of their young lives, might soon be winning this race, here was I at the end of my career without a single win to my credit, although I had been close to it many times.

The cavalcade moved off with Ferrari in front, then the red racing cars in single file, and the lorry with the mechanics. As we arrived at Brescia and forced our way through the crowds into the scrutineering enclosure in the Piassa della Vittoria. thousands of enthusiasts were milling around behind the barriers, craning their necks to see — and touch — the cars and the drivers. Soon their delight in the traditional contest would burst out from Brescia and spread throughout the roads of Italy. The cheers and good wishes continued all night as car after car left the ramp in the Viale Rebuffone. Meanwhile as the hour of our own departure drew near news came in about the speed of the early starters. The loudspeakers had some astonishing averages to announce: 115, 120, 125 mph.

I started with my mind made up. I had been chasing an outright win for many years, but luck had never come my way: in '49, in '52, '54, '55, and '56 I had stuck somewhere on that 1000 miles of road, fated not to reach the finish in that same Viale Rebuffone that I had left as dawn was breaking. In those years the winners had been Biondetti, Bracco, Ascari, Moss, and Castellotti; I had always had to stop, if only for a few seconds,

just when I was catching them up. It is true, of course, that luck enters into these open road races — but the luck had never been mine. Sometimes it was my own fault. Twice I crashed, with the Lancia and with the Maserati, but the other three times, always in the same make of car — Ferrari — I had stopped through a failure in the transmission — a part of the car that had always stood up perfectly well in other and even longer races. I began to wonder whether the fast but bumpy and undulating Mille Miglia course might be extra hard on the Ferrari transmissions, making them the Achilles heel of the cars from Maranello. I had also noticed the rear end jumping about a good deal, especially when an empty fuel tank had lightened the car. The bumping also coincided with certain parts of the course. I remember mentioning this several times in the notebook where I wrote down my post-race impressions.

In the 1957 Mille Miglia I set out feeling marvellous. I would not have changed places with any other driver in the world, whatever his name or reputation. I knew the course by heart and was very unlikely to mistake one corner for another — certainly not one of the 'key' corners. This was my strong point. For a given pace I could be certain of picking up at least a second on each of these 'key' corners and its succeeding straight. Over the whole race this would add up to five minutes, which could easily be a winning margin. I do not think any of my opponents had learned the course with such care. The best of them, like Moss, Collins, and de Portago, carried a companion who had repeatedly covered the course with them noting down all the tricky bits: the gulleys that were bad, and the ones that could be taken fast, the tricky corners, and so on. These notes they transcribed on to long rolls of paper from which they read out as they went along. A good idea, which had also been used by American drivers in the

Carrera Panamericana. Personally, I always preferred to rely on my memory, and in my later days I always drove alone.

On this twenty-fourth Mille Miglia my car bore the number 535, which to the crowds by the roadside signified the time of my departure from Brescia: 5.35 am. For me, however, it was a lucky number, because it added up to 13! I had also been lucky in the draw for starting times, for I was one of the last: von Trips was 5.32, Collins 5.33. Behind me there was no one formidable except Moss, and he retired shortly after the start when his brake pedal broke off. I caught von Trips before Pescara, 390 miles from the start, just as Collins completed his fill-up.

From the capital of the Abruzzo one starts on the central portion of the race; 405 miles between Pescara and Bologna, which entails two crossings of the Apennines, going to Rome and coming back, practically all of it on very twisty roads. This was the stretch where in previous years I had launched my attack, and often, by the end of it, come to grief; and it was here that I began to notice black tyre marks on the road, obviously left by some very potent motor-car indeed. It could only be Collins, as I had already passed von Trips, who had started ahead of me. Being absolutely determined to finish this time, I started the Pescara–Rome stretch with great care, and to spare the transmission I used the high gears as much as possible and avoided changing gear on the corners.

At Rome they said I had lost 5 minutes to Collins. So if I wanted to win I should have to hurry. I forced the pace up to 'ten tenths'; flat-out braking and low gear whenever corners forced me to slow. On acceleration, with the wheels bouncing clear of the ground, my rev-counter often went past the limit. I seemed to be following exactly in my opponent's black marks, and sometimes even

bettering his line, using all the width coming out of the corners. Even so, by the Viterbo depot 50 miles on I had not gained very much. Collins's pace was evidently the same as mine. I realised that even if I kept it up I could not catch him, and might well come unstuck as I had done before; and I seemed to have taken too many risks already.

In the last valley of the Apennines, between Florence and Bologna, the transmission started to make a nasty noise every time I revved up in the lower gears. 'This is it!' I thought, and felt thoroughly depressed: this year was going the same way as the others, and I should not even have had the satisfaction of leading the race. At the Bologna control it was raining. Ahead lay the long straight stretches of the Via Emilia, slippery in places. A few days before, while trying the car in the wet, I had found that if I tried to use full throttle in fourth at 125 mph severe wheelspin set in. To go faster than this the accelerator had to be used very gingerly – and so did the steering. Any sudden slowing could have made me lose control of the car. This being so, it seemed dangerous to go on: and suppose that on one of those fast straights the transmission trouble got worse, and suddenly locked the wheels? The Nurburgring incident in '35 came to my mind.

I had decided to stop, when I learned from Ferrari himself that 20 miles farther on the rain had stopped; and when I heard that Collins too had transmission trouble I got into gear and restarted. At that moment a loudspeaker announced that von Trips was passing through Livergnano, a hamlet 10 miles from Bologna. I tried to avoid gear-changing and to accelerate as gently as possible – which was fortunately easy as there are not many corners between Bologna and Brescia. I also kept down to 130 mph or so, which I could hold on half power. With less than 60

miles to go I began to glimpse a red car in the mirror, and soon afterwards it caught me up. It was von Trips. I made a rapid calculation: we still had about half an hour to go and at the moment I had a lead of 3 minutes: 10 per cent. If von Trips could average 12–15 mph more than me, he would win, and as there were no team orders he might well do so. Obviously Trips did not know about my gearbox, and I must see that he did not guess.

If I did not use my acceleration, and kept my speed down, he would certainly catch on. I speeded up to between 150 and 155 mph and waved him down; at which he obligingly stayed behind for a bit. Finally he made overtaking signs and came past. We were just coming to Piadena, a village 20 miles beyond Cremona. I remember the place exactly. I had made a special study of it, because it formed part of a special timed section

included in the race: the Gran Premio Nuvolari, a prize put up by the Automobile Club of Mantua, birthplace of the great Tazio, in his memory. This trophy was awarded for the best time on the 82-mile Cremona–Mantua–Brescia run — a section that it paid to learn, as, representing the last few miles of the race, it was the place where one might have to really hurry to fend off some late starter who suddenly appeared in one's mirrors. During practice I had done this run at daybreak when there was nothing about and I could go flat out in relative safety. I generally practised between four and seven o'clock, rather to the disgust of my wife, who always rode with me.

It so happened that very early one morning we had found ourselves in this village, and while waiting for a café to open we strolled up towards the square. Instinctively I took note of the 'S'-bend where the street curved right and then left. One came into the village down a long straight of about $2\frac{1}{2}$ miles. About 300 yards before the first right-hand bend of the 'S' there was a level-crossing, after which there were houses on each side of the road. To take the 'S's properly one had, after crossing the railway tracks, to pull over as far to the left as possible. I spotted that one could widen the road-space available by several yards by taking advantage of a sort of lay-by normally used by market lorries and carts. On the apex of the first bend there was a big house with a colonnaded portico and it seemed as though this would block the view down the street; but actually by looking through the outside arch, one could glimpse the line of the 'S', where its left-hand bend opened out slightly. On foot, standing beside the road I had noticed that the first bend was the slower because the sharper of the two: I should say about 105 mph for the one and 117 mph for the other. One could gain time by taking the first bend faster, by using the little lay-by. Then again 450 yards after the 'S's there was another 'blind' left-hander, also masked by a house. Our café was a long time opening so we drove on to look at this bend, and I judged from its angle that it was about 10 mph faster than the 'S's. It was the same with the next bend, and after the latter the road opened out and ran straight for more than three miles. With this detailed study in mind it should be easy, once through the 'S's in Piadena, to take the next two bends on the limit. We went back into the village and eventually got our *cappuccino*. It had been a most useful reconnaissance. Now back to the race.

As we approached Piadena, von Trips, who had been driving hard to shake me off, was about 200 yards ahead. As we came in sight of the village, about 100 yards from the level-crossing, he cut and I saw his brake lights come on. I realised I could pass. I did not move my foot from the

position I had been holding all this while, that is three-quarter throttle, and aimed the car hard left and across the lay-by, which, of course, on race day was empty. This almost doubled the width of the road: the normal 23 feet had become more like 40, and so I could take a much wider line. From this point, and looking down the road through the portico, the bend seemed to have straightened out.

I lifted very slightly 150 yards from the corner of the house and accelerated again at 50 yards so as to clip it as close as possible. From there on I did not lift at all, remembering that the next two corners were faster. As I came out of the last bend von Trips was only a few yards ahead, and I was able to pass him fairly easily on the run out. In those few bends I had not only wiped out von Trips's lead but also given him the impression that I was the better driver, at least over that stretch. I signed to take it easy, and he very sportingly did so. I did not know it yet, but those few bends had set the seal on my victory, the last and most coveted win of my life.

We reached the finishing line together, I still with my 3 minutes in hand. Just as the light of dawn had glinted on the bonnet of the last car to start, so the last rays of the setting sun greeted us on arrival. And in this appropriately twilight setting, my arrival produced a wave of genuine enthusiasm. At first I did not realise what it meant . . . It was all unfamiliar . . . Then dozens of people crowded round, hugging me, patting me on the back. When Isabella finally struggled through, escorted by policemen, as I was taking off my crash hat, I said how splendid it was to have actually finished for once. 'But you've won, darling!' she said. 'You've won!' And I, still not believing, made her repeat it again and again. I then learned that Collins, after leading for most of the race, had blown up 125 miles from the finish.

My joy in winning was clouded by the news which came in an hour later. Our team-mate de Portago, and his companion, Nelson, had been killed, together with nine spectators, in a dreadful accident. Thirty miles from Brescia a tyre burst and the car had left the road when travelling at 175 mph on the straight. Much has been written about this accident. When I heard the news I began to wonder. As one left Mantua there was an 'S'-bend, which could be straightened out if one cared to go off the asphalt of the road proper on to the granite setts forming the verge. Several seconds could be saved by taking this short cut, but there was a grave risk of damaging a tyre, should the wall strike the edge of one of the setts. I, too, had sometimes been tempted. One wonders whether perhaps de Portago may have damaged a tyre here, so that it burst later on the straight under the stress of high-speed running.

The following day I went to Modena to see Ferrari. To me it was no mere visit of thanks, but also one of condolence, although neither of us was any stranger to such tragedies. We did not exchange many words. I only remember his: '*Ingegnere*, I beg of you to remember your promise to your wife.'

7
Baron Huschke von Hanstein

MILLE MIGLIA
1940

I feel a little embarrassed already by this title, because I think I have never won a really great race myself, or even been one of the great racing drivers! On the other hand, I look back on nearly forty years of active racing, having won my first motor-cycle event as a student in England in 1929. I finished my career with two world records (10 kms and 10 miles) and four international class records (same distances) for the 2 litre and 3 litre class, at the VW test grounds at Ehra-Lessin in July 1973.

In all those years I was never really 'great', but probably more versatile than most other people, because I was active on motor-cycles of various shapes, makes, and sizes, as well as in grand touring, sporting, and racing cars. Furthermore, I tried my luck in all types of automobile sport — cross-country events, rallies, hill-climbs, long-distance, and circuit-races. I even signed a contract with the Auto-Union racing cars before World War II. But a mechanic drove me down a precipice, my right shoulder was crushed and still does not work properly, although I spent more than a year in a hospital. Thus my Grand Prix career was finished before it even started. What was left of power in that demolished arm was not strong enough to keep turning the wheel of the prewar 'Silver Arrows'.

Now, looking back at the many hundreds of events I have participated in, it is difficult to decide which I should call my greatest race. Memory calls back many happy and sad moments, which motor sport has brought into my life. But for many reasons my choice must be the Mille Miglia of 1940! Not only because it was the only one of the great classics I won overall, but also because the race itself was outstanding from many points of view.

It was the last race, before World War II generally stopped motor-racing. In addition, this race took place several months after the outbreak of war. For this reason the race became for Germany a matter of national prestige. It gave me a chance not only to leave Germany and go to Italy — which at that moment was still a neutral country — but also to see again many old friends who were officially supposed to be enemies. In fact, for reasons of security, the Italian government did not allow the Mille Miglia to be raced on the old classic route from Brescia to Rome and back. Instead, they had chosen a triangular course from Brescia to Cremona, to Mantua, and back on normal country roads, with a lap distance of just over 100 miles, which had to be covered nine times.

BMW, who were building at that time the famous 328 80-hp roadster, had decided to make three streamlined roadsters and two coupés on the basis of the 328, but developing about 120 hp, the top speed having been increased from about 160 km/h to 225 km/h. Naturally, competition among German drivers in that race was keen, especially for the open roadsters. Driving the coupés, one of which was built at BMW, the other one at Touring at Milan, seemed less attractive. In those days we did not know much about stabilisers, and the cigar-shaped coupés were extremely difficult to keep on the road! After some very nasty moments testing the cars on the Munich to Salzburg Autobahn the technicians gave me a chance to try one of the cars. At that time I had some experience with closed cars, having driven the streamlined Adlers several times in the 24-hour races at Le Mans and Spa.

Finally the team was made up of six German drivers in the open cars. Johnny Lurani and myself would drive one of the coupés and Franco Cortese and Walter Baumer, one of the young Mercedes-Benz factory drivers, the other. Having driven the cars down to Italy at that time it did not even enter our heads to put both sports cars on a lorry! — I had a first try-out on this circuit with Johnny Lurani. It may have been the zig-zagging of the car at high speed, or it may have been my way of driving, which at that time might still have been a little bit wild, anyway Johnny decided he would prefer not to go with me, but suggested we have one Italian and one German team.

So we changed partners. Baumer joined me, Johnny Lurani going with Franco Cortese. Our cars, of course, all had 2-litre engines, while our main opposition consisted mainly of eleven 2·5-litre Alfa Romeos, and two French 3-litre Delage cars. Internationally we were all relatively 'unknown' drivers, although I had been German champion in 1938. Our competitors on the other hand had big names like Farina, Biondetti,

44

Von Hanstein (third left) and his BMW team-
mates after the 1940 Mille Miglia.

Pintacuda, Sanesi, Conte Trossi, Comotti, and others.

As usual the Mille Miglia competitors started one by one. One-minute intervals beginning at four o'clock in the morning of 28 April 1940 separated 44 Fiat Topolino Ballila sports cars which were the first to shoot into the darkness. During the first lap we had a lot of trouble with fog in the Po Delta, but managed to take the lead 1 minute and 21 seconds in front of Comotti's Delage, followed by Lurani–Cortese in the second BMW and in front of the three Alfas of Farina, Biondetti, and Trossi. After three laps we should have changed drivers, but at that moment the competition was still so strong that when we reached the pits, about 25 km before Brescia, I was asked to press on and establish a bigger lead. In the meantime, the Lurani–Cortese coupé had stopped. Everything went well except that we had some difficulties with our normal brakes which were built to stop the car from the normal top speed of 160 and not from 220 km/h! Another difficulty was a stretch of gravel-road, which cut out the town of Mantua. Because of the dust and flying stones it was difficult to overtake slower cars. We were then afraid of breaking our windscreen, which would have destroyed completely the aero-dynamic nature of the car.

After 6 laps, about two-thirds of the race, I drove into the pits for our second scheduled stop and the car was filled up with petrol and oil.

This was the most tense and exciting stop of all for me. For poor Baumer, who had sat beside me patiently during the whole of the race, it was a bitter disappointment. He was young and keen and he was taking part in what we all knew was an historic race; the kind of event which would probably never be repeated because of the special conditions of war in Europe. It was a unique event in the calendar of motor-racing and Baumer had had to sit beside me, no doubt feeling he could have improved on my performance with every gear change, every twist of the steering wheel. I could see how tense he was when Alfred Neubauer, the legendary Mercedes-Benz racing director, took me on one side.

We were mingling with a whole galaxy of important people of the motor-racing world. Hermann Lang, the European champion, was a few feet away. Many of the BMW and Mercedes directors were watching the activities at the pits in this vital final stage of the race. Journalists and fans milled around as Neubauer told me urgently: 'You are used to the delicate machinery of the car now, we all think that we should keep the same driver or we may risk losing the overall winning place. Can you do it?' I answered immediately that I could. 'But what about Baumer?' I demanded. Neubauer waved this aside. 'We will give him a chance to cover himself with glory in the next race.'

Baumer was plainly very disappointed but obeyed orders and so we set off again with me in control and my patient co-driver beside me. I motored another 3 laps of this demanding 923-mile race and then pulled into the pits. Faces fell. There was consternation everywhere I looked in our pits. Some were beginning to swear and make despairing gestures. 'Now, at the very last lap of the race when we are in a winning position, something has to go wrong with the car.' I could almost hear their minds talking.

But I had a surprise planned. Not for the men in the pit, but for Baumer. He had endured nearly 1000 miles as my co-driver and I was determined he had the right at least to take the car over the finishing line. So for the last 20 km we changed seats and within a few minutes we were crossing the line, the very first drivers of a 2-litre BMW to win overall in one of the great classic races and the first time Germany had won the Mille Miglia

46

since the time of Rudi Caracciola. We had completed the course of 923 miles in 8 hours and 54 minutes at an average speed of a little over 106 mph. Our top speed had been about 125 mph.

I am sure it is not necessary for me to say how elated I was. To have won the Mille Miglia was a source of great satisfaction and pride for me, of course. But the aspect of the race which I remember thinking about then, and which often makes me pause even today, is that many of the hands which grasped mine as people congratulated me belonged to men who were supposed to be my enemies. Drivers and mechanics from other teams, famous journalists like Breadly and even Charles Faroux of *L'Auto*, the Paris journal, wrung my hand. Faroux, a dedicated enthusiast, had travelled to neutral Italy in time of war and there he was, officially my enemy, forgetting the war and concentrating on something which in those moments of excitement after a great race

was far more important! The fellowship of the circuit.

I believe it is this, rather than actually winning, which makes me choose the 1940 Mille Miglia as my greatest race. It proved more than any other race I have competed in that the camaraderie of motor sport and the friendships established among individual men are stronger than the foolish declarations of war made by impersonal governments.

I was happy. Baumer was happy too, having finally got his hands on the steering wheel and his feet on the pedals after nearly 1000 miles of frustrating inactivity! But I have to end on a sad note, for this was the last time he ever drove a racing car. He was killed in the war very soon after the Mille Miglia. However, it is some consolation to me that he is in the record books as the driver who took the winner of a unique classic race over the finishing line. As long as the race is remembered he will be remembered.

8
Jackie Stewart

GERMAN GRAND PRIX 1968

For Grand Prix drivers the German Grand Prix each year is a very special event because the Nurburgring is certainly the most difficult, the most treacherous, and the most demanding of the tracks that the circus travels to each year. Drivers are often asked what is their favourite circuit. In the majority of cases, they say that the Nurburgring is perhaps the most satisfying. This is said, in most cases, while sitting in armchairs in the comfort of their own homes with roaring fires in front of them! But really I don't believe that too many people would honestly admit that they enjoy driving on the Nurburgring in a Formula 1 car. I know that whenever I drive there I get back to the pits and take a big, deep breath because, My God, I'm pleased to be home! In 1968, that statement was

48

Jackie Stewart competing in heavy rain in the
1968 German Grand Prix.

Jackie Stewart in his Matra during the German
Grand Prix.

truer than ever as the Nurburgring was engulfed in a miserable fog and a steady drizzle soaked everyone.

I arrived at the Nurburgring late on Thursday afternoon after having flown up from Geneva with Graham Hill in his Piper Aztec, accompanied by Betty Hill, Jo Siffert, and Jo Bonnier. Just as we were unpacking the baggage from the plane the rain started, and from that point on we seldom got away from it. When we arrived at the 'Ring, which is some 30 km from the airport, I did 3 laps in a Volkswagen, taking my mechanic, Ken Tyrrell, and the Dunlop people around and on these 3 laps the circuit was dry all the way round. This was the only time I was going to see it that way during the entire week-end.

When official practice started on Friday morning I was starting my lightweight Matra on unscrubbed tyres and with new brake pads. The fog was extremely bad, with visibility down to 200 yards, but I did 15 laps of the short loop, bedding the tyres and brakes. By the time I had done this, the fog had got a little worse, and visibility had deteriorated round the back end of the circuit. As there was a practice session later in the afternoon, and another one on Saturday, Ken Tyrrell didn't think that it was a sensible move to risk the car under such conditions. At this time, certainly, flag marshals couldn't see each other and really the track was in no condition for racing. However, a few of the boys did go out, and had the advantage of a partly dry circuit although it was still very foggy. During this time Jacky Ickx, Chris Amon, Graham Hill, John Surtees, and Jochen Rindt put in some reasonably quick times that proved to be the fastest of the entire practice period. Vic Elford also put a quick lap in during that session. By the time the afternoon session was due to start, conditions had worsened if anything.

The organisers quite rightly said that conditions were far too bad to allow us out on the circuit so I didn't get out at all on Friday. This meant that we could only practise on Saturday, but then I did manage to put in a few laps in my car and recorded the fastest time of the day. However, everyone complained that there wasn't sufficient practice, and the officials decided that an early morning session on race day was a good idea. During this session I practised the car at long last with an aerofoil fitted, and found it to be slightly better. I cannot really say that it was noticeable while driving, but the times seemed to intimate that there was a slight improvement. But of course at the Nurburgring it is extremely difficult to recognise any small improvement in time. With the aerofoil on, I did record a time of 9 minutes 54·2 seconds which enabled me to get on to the third row of the starting grid. It is unusual at the Nurburgring to have a 3:2:3 grid; the normal thing there is to have 4:3:4, but in any case I would still have been on the third row of the grid.

When I did my fastest lap on the race morning, conditions really were very miserable. It was raining heavily, the fog was pretty bad in parts, and even then I don't believe the flag marshals could see each other. The rivers that were running across the track were the biggest problem for, on account of the trees, one cannot see pools of water as one usually can on most circuits, and all of a sudden one would arrive over the crest of a hill and go into a river that felt several inches deep and was probably 2 or 3 feet wide. The car would immediately aquaplane, and go out of control. On one occasion I was in top gear going along a straight piece of road when this occurred. The car went down the road sideways, flicked, and luckily came back pointing in the right direction. This sort of manoeuvre really isn't pleasant, and I came back to the pits to say that I didn't think that we should practise any more under these conditions, fearing that I might put a foot wrong on the morning of a Grand Prix, which would of course be pretty difficult to rectify. In fact, during this session, Jackie Oliver had such a moment, and was incredibly lucky to walk away from it because it was on an extremely slippery downhill section, entering a small bridge prior to the Adenauer Forest. Jackie got into some difficulties, knocked two wheels off the Lotus, and the Lotus mechanics performed absolute miracles to have the car roadworthy for the race which was due to start some $2\frac{1}{2}$ hours later.

The Grand Prix itself was started some 45–50 minutes later than scheduled. The engines were started at least 5 minutes before flag-fall, which was a mistake. Jo Siffert's engine certainly suffered from overheating during this spell, and John Surtees's motor certainly didn't improve itself, because John was alongside me on the grid and I could see that it was really boiling over. I could also see Graham was having trouble with water coming out of his car's overflow, and my temperature gauge was over 100 degrees Centigrade before we got fully under starter's orders.

When the flag did drop, Jackie Ickx made rather a poor start with too much wheelspin and I drove almost up the pit lane trying to get past him. I managed to do this but, in the process, got two wheels stuck in the gutter which drains the pit lane. It was quite a problem to get the car out of this position, and it felt rather like being stuck in the tram rails, so to speak: I just hoped that they didn't go to the tram depot!

Somehow, I found myself going into the first corner lying third behind Graham and Chris. The spray was absolutely unbelievable — I couldn't see anything at all! I couldn't see my braking distance marks; I couldn't see the car in front; it was just a great wall of spray. I tried to get out of the spray

and go up the inside, and by doing this I managed to see a little more clearly. I hate to think what was going on behind me! This situation continued for the majority of the lap, but I passed Chris Amon at the point almost where Jackie Oliver had his accident: that is to say, on the hill towards Adenauer. I was happy to do this because until then I cannot remember having been more frightened in a racing car. The spray from Graham and Chris was just absolutely impossible to see through; on any other circuit these conditions are hellish, but on the Nurburgring you just cannot imagine how bad they are. The track is narrow, the undulations so pronounced, the bends so numerous, that you can hardly remember where you are on the circuit even on a clear day, but in fog and ceaseless spray you just have no idea at all. In addition you are continually worried by the fact that you are aquaplaning and almost always losing control, and you feel sure that the man in front is doing the same thing so that at any moment he is going to appear just in front of you pointing in the wrong direction.

After passing Chris it was then a case of finding the right spot on the circuit to overtake Graham. This I dearly wanted to do before the start of the straight, so I managed to come out of the small Karussel at the end of the swallow-tail corner pretty well and I got an advantage on Graham at this point, overtaking him just entering the last corner before the straight. This meant that I had the complete home straight to myself without any hindrance from spray. With that alone I pulled out an advantage of over 8 seconds on Graham before reaching the pit. I knew what Graham was going through because at the speed reached on the straight, which was getting on for 170 mph, the spray was staying at road level for a tremendously long time due to the hedges keeping it back and of course with no wind, and the mixture of fog and

mist, you can imagine how impossible visibility was from behind.

After this it was only a matter of driving as fast as I possibly could because you simply can see nothing in your mirrors with so much spray around unless the next car is very close behind you. After 2 laps I had an advantage of 34 seconds or so and I managed to build up steadily on this, trying as hard as I could to stay on the road since there were so many times when one was almost sliding off, or hitting some new puddle that wasn't there on the previous lap.

With only 3 laps to go, it really started to pour down with rain all round the circuit, and the track became really treacherous. At a point about half a mile from the Karussel I entered an 'S'-bend in third gear and suddenly lost control in a deep river of water which was running across the road. The car immediately started sliding, the engine stalled, and I was hurtling across the road towards a marshal who was standing beside his post completely unprotected. He dived one way; then decided to jump the other way; then suddenly he just froze, and I knew I was going to hit him. But just then the wheels got a little bit of grip and I managed to regain control. Graham, in fact, who was some way behind, arrived at the same corner and spun off, but by this time the marshal had moved his position to somewhere a bit safer!

At last, I took the chequered flag just over 4 minutes ahead of Graham. It was a tremendously satisfying race to win, but I was very pleased to get it over with. I can remember thinking as I went down to the south turn after taking the chequered flag that this was perhaps my greatest ambition as far as winning on any circuit was concerned. The Nurburgring is a track on which I had always wanted to win a Grand Prix because I think it certainly is the greatest challenge to a driver, and I must say winning it in the rain was very satisfying. The car had gone like clockwork throughout and never missed a beat. It was a wonderful compliment to Ken Tyrrell's mechanics because the standard of workmanship that they had provided throughout the season was really splendid. The only trouble with the car at all during the race, apart from when it stalled, was that quite a lot of grit got into the throttle slides, and around half the distance the throttle was sticking open which really wasn't very convenient.

Even after winning such a race I can honestly say that I never felt that the GP would run the full distance. Each time I got back to the finish line I felt sure that the chequered flag was going to be shown, because really and truly the track was in no condition to be raced on. In fact, I think all the drivers deserve tremendous praise since, throughout the entire race, not one of them went off the track seriously enough to be injured.

9

Raymond Mays

INTERNATIONAL TROPHY AT BROOKLANDS 1936

In motor-racing, *Sa Sacrée Majesté le Hasard* delights in dealing out backhanders to his subjects, but in doing so he occasionally exercises a rough justice. On 2 May 1936, Prince Birabongse of Siam (B Bira) and I, central figures in what was probably the most dramatic race ever run at Brooklands, were both given the dirty end of a stick to hold. Bira, ignorant until after the finish that fate had been gunning for him, won the International Trophy at a record-breaking 91-mph average. Only too aware of *my* dose of fate's displeasure, I finished exactly 1 second behind the little Siamese after 260 miles of fast and furious racing.

But let's go back to the beginning.

To spare spectators 'the pain of thought', the

International Trophy was run under a uniquely simple handicap system. Instead of cars of different capacities being dispatched at precalculated intervals or given appropriate credit lap allowances, the track, at its widest point, was divided into five side-by-side chicanes of varying curvatures, or more exactly four chicanes and one straight and unobstructed channel. Then the field itself was broken down into five groups, and each group, once every lap, was routed through the chicane or channel befitting its theoretical speed capability. The smallest and slowest cars thus went through flat-out – no braking, no reaccelerating, no down – and up – shifting; the biggest and fastest ones executed a real dog-leg turn; and in-betweens had in-between wiggle-woggles to negotiate. To discourage drivers from entering this critical zone at speeds that might lead to side-swiping contact with others in neighbouring chicanes, it was immediately preceded by a compulsory-for-everyone, slowing-down channel, its flanks delineated, like those of the handicap *Skaggeraks*, by marker barrels linked together with bunting-hung ropework.

The International Trophy circuit, incidentally, was traversed clockwise, opposite to the Brooklands norm, and measured 2·6 miles per lap. The course included the Byfleet Banking and the tangential Finishing Straight (a section not normally used since the track's earliest days) but cut out the Home Banking. Starters in this 1936 event, fourth in the series, numbered 42, their cars ranging from tiny supercharged Austin Sevens to 2·9-litre Grand Prix Alfa Romeos. Out of the 42 hopefuls who went into battle on that memorable 2 May, 27 were to fall by the wayside, or Weyside, for the little Wey River meanders through the Brooklands precincts and is actually spanned by the circuit at two points.

Most fancied runners out of the 42 were two perfectly matched and almost identical $1\frac{1}{2}$-litre ERAs – Bira's Romulus, painted bright blue, Siam's national racing colour, and my green car.

The lead and next-up places changed hands repeatedly during the early and middle stages, with Harry Rose (GP Maserati), Bira, Cyril Paul (ERA), Hector Dobbs (Riley), and myself taking turns to head the jockeying, tyre-screaming cavalcade. Unknown to almost everybody outside our two camps, there was just one significant difference between Bira's ERA and mine: his had an oversize fuel tank which, according to careful pre-race checks, would enable him to run 20 laps further before a fill-up became necessary. As, however, his extra range wasn't going to give him a non-stop run, but merely postpone the bunkering operation, his advantage was a doubtful one. (Contemporary reports and subsequent analyses of the race, incidentally, stated that I had the benefit of a power-boosting Zoller supercharger, though actually mine was of the same Jamieson type as Bira's.)

I duly made my tanking stop well before him – at 50 laps, half-distance. Bira was leading and I was second at this stage; my halt stretched his lead to 102 seconds and let Dobbs and Rose up into second and third spots. Well, I wasn't worried about Dobbs or Rose, and as for Bira, he, after all, was going to have to stop and refill eventually . . .

Prince Chula, Bira's cousin and manager, was as usual in charge of the Siamese depot and personally displaying what were known as his worm-in-agony pit signals, couched in Siamese characters and thus guaranteed to be indecipherable by Occidental rivals. But the orders he issued to his pit staff as the time approached for Bira's fill-up were totally uncharacteristic of him. With his precise and penetrating mind and eye for the minutest detail, he had always worked on the principle that the advance study and correct interpretation

Raymond Mays leading the 1936 International
Trophy, Brooklands.

of regulations were as vital to success as the driver's personal skill and the raceworthiness of his car.

Now the International Trophy rules laid it down that, during pit stops, *two men*, and no more, were permitted on the track. So, when Romulus came to a tyre-smoking standstill, Bira, on prior instructions, stayed where he was in the cockpit while two mechanics threw themselves into their well-rehearsed tanking routine. An official immediately spotted the infringement and dashed on to the scene, shouting to Prince Chula to unblot his copybook fast, or else. (Lapping at over 90 mph, I had no idea until afterwards, of course, of what was afoot. The same goes for many other incidents which, for simplicity's sake, I am describing as from an eye-witness's viewpoint.)

Momentarily incredulous, Chula nevertheless didn't argue the point. He ordered one mechanic back behind the pit counter, leaving his mate to complete the job single-handed.

The seconds lost while this *bruhaha* was being sorted out were serious for the White Mouse Stable, as the royal cousins called their little *scuderia*, but a by-product of it was more serious still. With the taut thread of his concentration stretched to snapping point, Chula muddled his lap chart and inadvertently credited Dobbs and me with one more lap than we'd actually done.

The fact that he'd done this wasn't and couldn't be known to rival pit managers but a suspicion of it gradually dawned on Humphrey Cook, the philanthropist and former racing driver in his own right, who had financed the ERA venture and was managing my pit with Peter Berthon, the ERA designer. It dawned, too, on Dr Dudley Benjafield, founder of the British Racing Drivers' Club, who was a non-competitor that day and enjoying his neutral role as he strolled around the pit area and watched points.

It suddenly struck Benjy that Bira, for no apparent reason, was going round about a second per lap slower than before his petrol stop, and Chula wasn't doing a thing to speed him up. The only possible explanation was that Chula thought I had a clear lap's lead over his man, making his task an impossible one: better a safe second place than a possibly expensive blow-up in pursuit of an uncatchable quarry.

With no axe to grind either way, Benjafield spelt out the situation to Chula, but in vain. Chula's lap charting had never failed him yet and he simply couldn't believe it was doing so now. He thanked Benjafield courteously but let the situation stand.

Having done his best to cook the Siamese goose, *Sa Sacrée Majesté* turned his fire on me. With 90 laps covered I was leading the race (albeit less commandingly than Prince Chula imagined), with Bira second, half a minute to the bad, and Dobbs third, the best part of 3 minutes down. Then my troubles started. A telltale spluttering, the dreaded symptom of fuel starvation, interrupted the clean blare of my ERA's exhaust note. Hoping against hope that I was mistaking the fault, and that by some miracle all six cylinders would regain their old harmony, I switched over to reserve fuel supply, pressed on for 2 more laps, then drew despairingly into the pit.

The tank was indeed almost dry, for a reason which again was to be a mystery until after the finish: fuel had been leaking through a split opened up in the tank by the battering that all cars suffered over the bumpy Brooklands surface.

The stop was a short one — no point in taking aboard a whole tankful at this stage of the game, leak or no leak; but, precisely as Bira roared past into the lead, one of the Dunlop mechanics tugged at Peter Berthon's sleeve and pointed to my offside rear tyre. It was treadless, worn right down to the breaker strip.

There were two courses open to us and the problem was all mine: should we change the wheel and bid a final farewell to any chance of winning, or race on and risk a blow-out which at worst might send the car careering up and over the high Byfleet Banking at 140 mph? Emerson, philosopher and poet, said, 'Always do what you're afraid of doing', and in many crises I have found this precept a sound one. I was afraid to press on, knowing that my life might depend on that already thin and progressively deteriorating tyre, so I pressed on.

Meanwhile, at the pits, Cook had added his voice to Benjafield's with assurances to Prince Chula that the two ERAs were indeed on the same lap. Bira's, it's true, was now leading the race as the result of my unscheduled pit stop, but as long as he continued to think he was lying a poor second he obviously wasn't going to pull out all the stops.

It was this tip-off from Cook, who certainly did have an axe to grind, that finally unblinkered Chula's eyes. If Chula's one serious rival said the race order was Bira/Mays, not Mays/Bira, thereby voluntarily exposing his own driver to the danger of Bira/Mays finishing order, then who could doubt it?

Now at last all the cards were on the table, business side up. Spectators in the public enclosures, knowing only what they were told over the tannoys, had little inkling of the high drama of a race that was to take its place in the hymnals of motor-racing.

But the pit-area *cognoscenti* didn't need a knowledge of Siamese to understand the SPEED UP import of the signal held and waved aloft by Prince Chula. His feelings at this moment of truth, as he afterwards told me, were mixed — a compound of bitter self-blame for a mistake that might have cost Bira the race, with almost incredulous gratitude towards Humphrey Cook for one of the most sporting actions ever taken in motor-racing.

That final eight-lap fight to a finish is something that personally I'll never forget. The International Trophy course, unlike many circuits, including some of the other Brooklands go-rounds, had the peculiarity of giving the driver an uninterrupted view of the whole perimeter from any given point. I thus found myself in the role of a human computer, measuring the closing gap between Bira and myself lap by lap, almost furlong by furlong, and mentally calculating my chances of catching him in the precious, dwindling minutes that remained. With the other half of my mind I was debating, with a curious sort of detachment now, whether that ever-weakening back tyre would stand the punishment it was taking as the ERA clawed for lateral grip on the alternate right- and left-hand swerves through our handicap chicane, on the long sweep of the steep Byfleet Banking and, worst of all, in the battle with centrifugal force where the Railway Straight terminates in a right-hand dive off the Wey Viaduct and down over some of the roughest of the Brooklands concrete into the Finishing Straight.

At times like this one's mind acquires a stop-watch-like perceptiveness, and to my joy it told me that a second here, a fraction of a second there, was being won and held. Yard by yard, foot by foot, the distance between the blue car and the green contracted. As they pulled out of the chicane area, throwing up spurts of concrete dust from their spinning back wheels, to start the hundredth and last lap, Romulus was ahead by a few lengths. Round the banking I crept up and up on Bira, drew level where the banking levelled out, and finally inched into the lead on the short Railway Straight, not much more than a kilometre from the finish. For both of us, every nerve was strained, throttle pedals were hard to the floorboards.

Gordon Crosby's painting of one of the most exciting races ever staged at Brooklands: the 1936 duel between Raymond Mays (right) and Prince Bira.

Then it happened. On the last corner of this, the very last lap, my engine fluffed momentarily on one cylinder. As I was later to learn, a sparking plug had cut out, then in again, in a half-hearted way. Bira, with full power available as an aid to steering, wrenched Romulus lower on the climbing, cross-banked turn and nipped inside me. With my front axle level with his rear wheels, we tore along the Finishing Straight, peering through fly-spattered screens at the chequered flag which we could clearly see held and brandished aloft by an official (I even remember he was wearing a long overcoat and a trilby hat!).

Down swung the black and white symbol of victory in a fluttering sweep. Bira was the winner, by a solitary second in 260 miles. *Sa Sacrée Majesté* had pronounced his verdict. Just for good measure he threw in a little joke: 100 yards beyond the finishing line, Romulus burst his gearbox. To the Junior Car Club, organisers of the International Trophy, I suppose 100 laps sounded a nice round figure. Too bad — for me — they hadn't made it 101.

10
Froilan Gonzales

BRITISH GRAND PRIX
1951

More than twenty years have passed since that British Grand Prix and yet it seems to me as if it was yesterday. It needs only a casual word at a party, a friend or perhaps a journalist asking me, 'How was it all in the beginning, Pepito?', for memories to flood into my mind; memories of a raw, inexperienced lad from Argentina.

Since then I have received praise and congratulations from kings, princes, and statesmen in many countries. I have forgotten many races. But always fresh in my mind is 14 July 1951.

It really began earlier when I was, for my local countrymen, still Cabezon (Big Head!) Gonzales, a driver who was content to win on local dirt circuits, thinking of no more exalted arenas. Then Don Francisco Borgonovo, President of the Racing

Gonzales in his Ferrari during the 1951 British Grand Prix.

Board of the Argentine Automobile Club, telephoned me at the beginning of 1950, asking if I would join the team which the Club were sending to Europe, under the leadership of my great friend and countryman, Juan Manuel Fangio. I accepted of course, but was very unlucky that year and did nothing spectacular. The Club were patient with me and selected me for 1951, however.

I was at Reims, ready to race in the 1951 Grand Prix de France in a Maserati owned by the Argentine Automobile Club, when something happened which changed my destiny. Nello Ugolini, then director of the Ferrari team, asked me if I could drive one of the team cars because their driver Dorino Serafini had been injured in the Mille Miglia. The request, I learned later, came from Don Enzo Ferrari himself. I was astonished that a 'peasant' of very little experience could have at-

tracted the notice of the great Ferrari. We all held him in awe and I can recall, even now, my stumbling excitement as I agreed. I had few illusions about my chances but from that moment I seemed to be living in a dream and even when they took me to the workshop to be measured for the seat and for the pedals I still could not believe I was to be the driver of Ferrari's mechanical jewel. I was nervous, happy and afraid at the same time, like a peasant who suddenly attains the love of a princess.

The dream was to be very brief. I was utterly determined to make my mark at Reims in the Grand Prix de France and after a tough battle I managed to lead the race. But when I stopped at the pits to refuel Ugolini told me to hand over my jewel to Alberto Ascari who had walked back to the Ferrari pits after his own car had broken down.

62

Recalling it now I suppose it was understandable. Ascari was more experienced in the Grand Prix arena than I. And, since he was now available, it was obviously more sensible to let him take over. But at the time I was mystified and wounded. I assumed I had in some way failed one of Ferrari's mysterious tests. Yet nobody would tell me where I had failed.

I was just as puzzled when Enzo Ferrari sent for me. Puzzled and timid. For Ferrari was a powerful experienced man of the world while I had only recently arrived in Europe. I had no idea how to address the 'sacred monster' of the motoring world when I was led into his office. I managed to say 'Good morning' in Spanish and then I stood there speechless, wondering why I was there and what to do next. Don Enzo, realising my embarrassment, helped me out by smiling and shaking my hand. And to my utter amazement he — the greatest figure in world motor-racing — actually congratulated me for what I had done at Reims. I was even more astounded when he suddenly asked me: 'Would you like to sign a contract to drive for the Ferrari team?' I can feel even now the almost painful thumping of my heart. This just isn't true, I told myself.

Plainly Ferrari was aware that he had confused me for he continued by saying that the terms of my contract would be the same as those for Villoresi and Ascari, his official drivers. But this did not matter to me. I was hardly listening to the details. I think I was already holding a pen — ready to sign anything. I only wanted to race, to become part of the powerful Italian team which seemed to me like attaining the highest rung of the ladder. After a very short career in motor-racing I had attained the equivalent of singing at La Scala, Milan.

Ferrari had the gift of instilling confidence in his drivers. Although I was still very inexperienced I arrived at Silverstone for the 1951 British Grand Prix feeling that I really belonged in the Scuderia Ferrari, feeling eager also to pit my car's power against the almost unbeatable Alfa Romeos — and my own skill against the world's greatest racing drivers. Silverstone was the meeting place for international statesmen, industrialists, and millionaires, all looking for excitement.

During practice I had broken Farina's lap record so I shared pride of place on the first row of the starting grid beside Fangio and Farina in Alfa Romeos and Ascari, my team-mate, in a Ferrari. I felt very much that we were in the public eye — just as I had at Reims — but this time I knew that nobody would take my car away from me.

The 'jewel' was at the starting grid while I kept pacing back and forth under tremendous nervous tension. I wandered aimlessly in a daze while a handful of my countrymen — just a few of my own people in this crowded and very foreign arena — were talking to me, trying to calm me. I could not listen to them. My mind would not concentrate on anything but the race. It was my obsession. I even carried on a conversation with myself: 'Pepito! You, a peasant, have entered a high society party.' I tried to relieve tension by asking myself: 'Pepito! What are you doing among so many Field Marshals? What will they all say in Argentina, in Arrecifes; what will your parents think?' And finally, when these questions did nothing to calm my nerves, I muttered aloud in a panic: 'Pepito! How will you get out of this!'

It was the strident note of the horn announcing 5 minutes to race time which brought me abruptly to my senses. I had to rush to the toilet! And each time that devilish horn sounded again it increased my tension and anxiety. But at last we were in our cars. I stared at the starter, very careful not to move my car a fraction of an inch forward, since an early start meant a one-minute penalty. All the engines were revving impatiently while the crowd stood motionless watching us all on the grid. To me the grid was Hades and the engines were instruments in a hellish concert. My heart felt as if it would burst. Breathing was difficult. Then, just before I felt that I must pass out, the starter's flag came down. We were away. And what a start it was. The four of us in the front row, trying to lead the pack, accelerated so suddenly that our wheels spun while the cars moved forward in slow motion, leaving behind a cloud of rubber smoke through which the other cars roared, overtaking us like arrows! When our tyres got a grip on the track we found that instead of being pursued we were pursuing, trying desperately to find a gap in the crush of vehicles to catch up the leaders who were, of course, increasing their speed.

As we passed the pits for the first time I noticed that both the Alfa and Ferrari team managers were signalling the same instructions, which were in effect that we should drive our own race. The alarming start had meant that team tactics must be abandoned. 'Go for the lead,' came the urgent message and as soon as I saw that I went flat-out. By the next lap I was leading.

I could not hear them but I had the feeling that the British crowd had forgotten their usual restraint. They were jumping and waving and, it seemed to me, yelling like mad. 'Pepito. You are ahead of the Field Marshals,' I thought, and kept my foot hard down on the accelerator pedal. Then suddenly my rear-view mirror showed a red car, growing bigger and bigger. A signal from my pit as I shot past told me that it was Fangio's Alfa Romeo. 'Pepito. Don't do anything foolish. Don't panic. Even Fangio will have to re-fuel.'

When Fangio caught me in the 10th lap I let him overtake, placing myself directly on his tail. We travelled in tandem, our two cars seeming to be roped together. Even when he increased speed

we remained like this, driving like men pursued by the Devil himself. There was a moment of danger around the 25th lap when I took Becketts Corner too fast and hit the straw bales. But this made me keener than ever and I set off again after Fangio. I began to close on him, having been perhaps 5 or 6 seconds behind him with both of us averaging about 97 mph until, on the 39th lap, I eventually took him. Towards the end of the race I was more than a minute ahead of him. I knew that he could not possibly make up 10 seconds per lap, although I thought he was trying. I even looked over my shoulder as I eased up a little. Within a few laps after that I saw the chequered flag waving for me. I had won my first Grand Prix.

I drove the winner's lap and then, nearing my pit, I saw my mechanics jumping, waving their arms. The spectators were standing. When I stopped I was lifted bodily from the car. My wife, Amalia, hugged me and then friends rushed forward to embrace me: Corner, Fernando, Guzzi, the Argentine Ambassador Hogan; all their faces were blurred as they surrounded me, encircling me in such a strong embrace that I still feel their warmth and the moisture of their tears mingling with mine. All around us was confusion and excitement. 'The Alfa Romeos are beaten', the mechanics were shouting as they handed me a drink and solicitously cleaned my face.

After a few minutes they led me forward, a compact little group, to the presence of the Queen of England who congratulated me. I was crowned myself — with a wreath of laurels. From all sides I heard cries I did not understand. I saw hands trying to reach me and heard words in many languages, but none in my own tongue. It was strange music, but very pleasing to my spirit.

Then I was carried to the winner's podium. All became quiet. People were still as they faced towards me. The deep silence was broken by the

first chords of the Argentine National Anthem. It was the first time that I had been the centre of such a touching ceremony; and I started crying when I saw my country's flag being hoisted to the top of the winner's standard.

I was young, a country boy. And now more than twenty years have gone by. But I still remember July 1951 and often find myself again in that turmoil of hands, voices, and cries which, if I close my eyes, I can still see and hear around me . . .

Gonzales' victory in the 1951 British Grand Prix ended the long run of Alfa Romeo triumphs.

11
Innes Ireland

SOLITUDE GRAND PRIX 1961

Now, just which was my greatest race? Was it my very first race, driving a motor-car around a circuit in competition with other drivers — the race which gave me an introduction to the sport in which I had dreamed of becoming involved since I was a boy? Was it the race which gave me the most pleasure, or was it the one which brought me the greatest public acclaim? The one which made me the first Scotsman ever to win a Grand Prix? The race which gave Lotus their first win with a single-seater racing car — or any one of dozens of others which I remember on the occasions when I think back to my racing days? Perhaps it was the last race I drove, the one which finally made me decide that this phase of my life was over.

It is a difficult choice to make, and I am sure

that the word 'great' will have a different meaning for each of the drivers who contributes to this volume. When I really think about it, every race was 'great'. They were all fun, and each had a place in my racing career, if my ten years of fun can be called that. The early days driving my Lotus Mk II were perhaps the friendliest, for most of the events were in club meetings run by the British Automobile Racing Club at Goodwood. At the end of the season the Brooklands Memorial Trophy, presented by *Motor Sport*, was awarded to the driver who had accumulated the greatest number of points in the series of races. The meetings themselves had a splendid atmosphere but this did not diminish the fierce rivalry between drivers.

Throughout the season Keith Green in his Cooper, Chris Bristow in his similar car, and I, battled it out wheel-to-wheel. It was all good, clean fighting, every inch of the way. I held a slender lead over my adversaries until the last race and, so long as I finished third at worst, I should win the trophy. But second and third places were not quite so secure. If Bristow came first or second he would take second overall, and the same could be said for Green.

Caution dictated that I should just drive a steady race and be content with a safe third place, making certain that I stayed on the road right to the finishing flag. However, caution was not one of my greatest attributes and I had somehow got the reputation of 'Ireland will win, or at least he'll be in front when he flies off the road!' I'd won most of the races so far, and when the flag dropped for this last one I was just as determined to win it — and to hell with caution and coming a steady third.

I was inches in front all the way, until the last corner of the last lap. I was never one for getting on the brakes too early, but in spite of this, Chris Bristow came hurtling past me on my inside just as I started to turn into the corner. He hadn't a hope of ever staying on the road, but it was a jolly brave attempt to win. I didn't even alter my line and, sure enough, by the time I got to the apex, there was Chris throwing up great clods of earth and dirt as he struggled to avoid the banking, his poor Cooper scrabbling for grip as it went sideways and backwards and in most other directions. This, of course, let Green into second place and that was the order for the Brooklands Memorial Trophy.

I was particularly proud of myself, for this award had previously been won by my great hero, Mike Hawthorn, and it was Mike who had been asked to present the award on this occasion. The only drawback to having my hero present me with the trophy was that he drank most of the champagne which was poured into the cup, twice coming up for air!

To some extent, great races are decided by great cars. While the D-Type Jaguar was not the fastest car in its class by the time I raced one, I was thrilled when asked to do so. One of the reasons was that I was invited to drive one of those beautiful machines by my national team, Ecurie Ecosse, who had done so much for Jaguar by twice winning at Le Mans. I drove for the team on several occasions, the most memorable of these being at Le Mans in 1959.

I was to share a car with the American driver, Masten Gregory, he being Number One. The team manager asked me if I would mind towing one of the caravans to the circuit so, *en route* for Dover, I picked it up in South London. Having done a fair bit of towing trailers around the Continent, I was a bit put out when I found that our sleeping quarters for the race were contained within the walls of a 22-foot-long monstrosity that was bound to swing about like a ship in a following sea if towed at anything over 30 mph. Inwardly groaning at the thought of the trip ahead I set off to catch the boat.

In fact, the thing towed better than I had expected, and was reasonably stable at 40 mph. This, of course, encouraged me to go that bit quicker and, so long as I was accelerating, it wasn't too bad. Braking and cornering were a bit hectic and there were occasions when I was half-way up the next bit of straight, steering frantically in all directions, before I got the 'thing' back to some semblance of control. The French roads gave us a fairly rough ride, and over the humps and bumps car and caravan heaved and pitched in an alarming manner. The final crunch came when I rounded a corner to find a very rough-looking level-crossing just at the foot of a fairly steep incline. We fairly leapt on to the crossing and the downward lunge was accentuated by the immediate incline. As the car started up this, the caravan was still going down — and with some force. There was the most appalling noise as everything, including the back of my car, hit the road surface, and the rebound was just as alarming. The next few hundred yards were covered in what might be described as a lame kangaroo hop.

I didn't really want to know how much damage had been done, and since Le Mans wasn't too much farther up the road, we carried on. Eventually, we pulled up behind the pits, breathing sighs of relief as we started to unhitch the 'thing'. The first problem arose when we tried to screw down the jacks to level the van; the front ones were bent backwards and under the floor, as was the jockey wheel. But worse was to come. Someone opened the door — and most of the interior of the van poured out on to the grass. Beds had fallen out of their fittings, lamps off the walls, a pile of broken gramophone records crunched under foot, and the kitchen area looked as if the IRA had taken a dislike to it. The cooker itself seemed to have disintegrated, doors and trays were all over the floor, together with most of the sections of the decorative tiling off the walls around cooker and sink. I left for my hotel with some haste!

For Masten and I the race in itself was not a great success, although I did move up to second place at one stage. Shortly before midnight on the Saturday the engine blew up and we went back to the pub for a good meal and a good night's sleep. It was Aston Martin's year, their DBR.I cars taking first and second places. Stirling Moss was in their team, although he, too, had spent his night in bed after his car broke down. He did, however, write a book on this particular race and in it he dealt at some length on the benefits of practising the famed Le Mans start.

To illustrate his point, he showed two full pages of photographs with various shots of the action from the drop of the flag until getting under way. These showed him and the driver next to him leaving their places well before most of the others had even reached their cars. As it happened, I was in the car next to Stirling, and he complimented me by including me in all his remarks. As I have said, his main point was that by practising the start and getting under way as quickly as possible, one was off without being tangled up in the mêlée of the main pack of cars, thereby saving valuable seconds.

I clearly remember my session of practice of the start. The ignition switch and starter button were located very close to each other, so my plan was simple. Before my bottom could reach the seat I would switch on the ignition with my left hand and, since the car would be left in first gear, I would depress the clutch pedal as I slid down into the seat. A split second after the ignition was on I would press the starter, the engine would fire and I would be off. The only thing left to do was to practise the whole operation.

One morning before official practice, I went to our garage to find my car all ready and parked with its tail towards the wall in just the right position for a Le Mans start. Carefully I measured the distance of the track away from it, gave myself an imaginary drop of the flag, and sprinted for the car. As I reached the car my right hand landed just in front of the windscreen, I leapt in the air twisting around as I did so, cleared the screen and slithered down into the seat, going through all the motions I have outlined. I got out of the car and went through the whole process again. I think I managed three of these practice runs before Sandy, one of our mechanics, appeared on the scene. I thought I might be greeted with a show of enthusiasm for my diligence but his broad Scots voice shouting, 'Hey, Innes, what the bloody hell do you think you're doing? You'll break the bloody windscreen,' put paid to any further perfection of my technique. So much for Stirling and his constant Le Mans practising. Maybe the Aston mechanics didn't care if he broke *their* bloody windscreen . . .

But it was still a great event for me. I was very proud to be a member of such a famous team and it was thrilling to be in charge of such a marvellous piece of machinery as the D-Type Jaguar. Since it had been designed for Le Mans it was particularly good on this circuit. And it was fast. Down the straight it would do about 175 mph and it would do it in such a well-behaved way, running as straight as a die with just a light hold on the wheel. With practice, the kink, as we called it, near the end of the Mulsanne Straight, could be taken flat out, although one did have to use all the road and get the correct line to avoid finishing up on the grass — not a good idea at 175 mph. Braking for the very slow corner at the end of the straight was memorable, for the exhaust note of

the 'D' on the over-run under heavy braking was music to the ears, and the blip of the engine as one changed down through the gears was enough to set the blood tingling in one's veins. I often wanted to be a spectator at this point just to be able to watch and listen as the car lost speed from 175 mph to about 30 mph.

And what a lesson in gamesmanship I learned from Roy Salvadori, one of the Aston Martin drivers! As the race settled down, I was lying about fifth or sixth, with Salvadori behind me. We circulated like this for lap after lap, and I noticed that I had the legs on him down the straight although he did manage to gain a considerable amount of speed in my slipstream. If anything, the Aston was slightly quicker around the corners, but by taking the Dunlop Bridge past the pits flat-out — which was just possible — I managed to hold my place in front of Roy. After a couple of hours of this, Salvadori started flashing his lights at me as we swept through the 'S's before the Mulsanne Straight. He would flash them again in the braking area at the end of the straight. He kept up this flashing business for several laps. I couldn't believe that he had the extra speed to keep in front of me but eventually I thought I ought to let him through. I eased off early at the end of the Mulsanne and waved Roy past on my inside. As he went by I glanced over at him to suffer the frustration of seeing him laughing his head off as he gave me a cheerful wave. Talk about being out-fumbled! I later learned that Roy was a past-master at this art, but I did get my own back on him a year or two later at Silverstone.

One race that gave me a great deal of personal satisfaction was the 1961 Solitude Grand Prix for 1·5-litre Grand Prix cars. This race was not a World Championship event although all the contenders for the series were there. I was driving for Team Lotus with Jim Clark, our cars being fitted

Ireland's Lotus 21 leading Bonnier's Porsche at Solitude in 1961.

with the 1·5-litre 4-cylinder Coventry-Climax engines. The main opposition came from a very strong team of four works cars from Porsche who were obviously determined to win on their home ground. Their team included Bonnier, Gurney, and Hermann.

Solitude is the most beautiful of circuits, and could be described as a miniature Nurburgring. It has many corners, ups and downs, and runs through beautiful wooded country. The last section of the course runs from the end of the straight back to the pits with something like eighteen 'S'-bends one after the other, these making it very difficult for cars of equal performance to pass one another. For me, this was the crucial part of the course.

On paper, Porsche stood the best chance of winning, for their chassis was exceptionally good and their engine was putting out considerably more horsepower than our Climax unit. But, more important still, they had much better torque which would help them out of corners and uphill. But in Team Lotus we had our own secret weapon — our new tyres. Dunlop had developed a new type specifically designed for wet weather; it had a softer rubber mix which gave increased adhesion, but greatly reduced life.

Naturally, we kept very quiet about this tyre, but I did try them out during practice and managed to get on to the front row of the grid — I may even have been in pole position. They were obviously a success, even in the dry, and gave me greater cornering powers. It was a gamble whether or not the tyres would last the race in dry conditions, for it was over 26 laps of the circuit, giving a total distance of 190 miles or so. But it was a gamble we took and, as my car was rolled out on to the grid in almost perfect weather conditions, the give-away green spots could clearly be seen on the walls of my tyres.

Making a good, clean start with the Climax engine was no easy matter, but I got everything just right as the flag dropped and swept into the first corner inches ahead of Bonnier and the rest of the pack. Up the hill in second and off into the woods I maintained my lead, and by the time we got to the long straight I was delighted to find that I was about 150 yards ahead. Relentlessly Bonnier ate up the gap and, by the time we got to the second-gear corner at the end of the straight, he was snapping at my heels. This corner was a tight one to the right, followed almost immediately by a hairpin to the left, a short burst around a right-hander and then another, slower, left-hander — all downhill — and then off on the crucial section of high-speed swerves back to the pits about two miles away.

Again my tyres helped me a bit, and by the time we got to the pits I was about 30 yards in front. This went on for lap after lap; I would pull out a lead through the corners, only to have it reduced to nothing on the straight. Try as I might, I could never get far enough away to be comfortable.

The pack behind me consisted of Bonnier, Gurney, Brabham, McLaren, Moss, and Hermann, and they all took turns at being second. I had settled down to the realisation that this was how the race would be run, and as long as my car held out — and as long as I got round the corners at the end of the straight first — then I should manage to win the event. This situation had not escaped the chaps behind and they were all still there — with the exception of Stirling who had dropped out — and trying to do something about it.

I had a rude awakening on lap 19 when Brabham shot past the car on my tail as we approached the braking area at the end of the straight — and, what's more, he shot past me as well. I had a taste of my own medicine for a while as I desperately looked for a way past old Jack (actually he wasn't so old then!). I realised that I would have to find a way long before we got to the straight, otherwise he would hold me up round the corners and neither of us would get far enough in front of the Porsche pack to stay ahead by the end of the straight.

Fortunately, I found a way past by coming round the corner at the start of the uphill section just after the pits, considerably faster than Jack, and out-accelerated him up the hill. With any luck, I thought, he would hold up the Porsches for a bit on the twisty parts.

Unbeknown to me, the organisers had arranged a system whereby the national flag of the car in the lead would be raised at the end of each lap. The Union Jack had flown proud for 24 laps, and so it remained until the penultimate lap. Bonnier managed to stay right on my tail – and I mean right on it – all along the fast section from the end of the straight; he had obviously worked out his tactics as well! From the last corner there was a straight of perhaps 300 yards to the start–finish line, and as we accelerated from the corner, Jo came out of my slipstream and accelerated past. There was just nothing I could do about it. So up went the German flag at last, there to be tied very firmly with a typically thorough German knot. The chap operating the flag had decided the order of things! However, Chapman and I had other ideas. Apparently Chapman's remark to our pit was: 'Well, either Innes is going to win or we'll never see him again!'

Bonnier was really giving his Porsche the stick, and all I could do was to stay right on his tail. Once on the straight his slipstream gave me quite a tow, but I still lost a few precious yards. The thing was going to be decided in the braking area. I knew that I could outbrake Jo, but I didn't want to show my hand too soon. Just as we got to the point where Jo should be getting on the brakes, I pulled out to the right, my foot still hard on the floor. Jo was watching my every move, and as I pulled out, so did he. But I had to go on, for there wasn't time to swing back to his inside. With my foot still on the floor, I was on the grass on the right of the road wondering just when in heaven's name was Jo going to get on the brakes!

With the corner getting perilously close at last I saw the nose of the Porsche dipping hard. I got back on to the road and then set about trying to get myself slowed down, being well past my braking marker. It was panic stations, all right, and my poor Lotus didn't quite know which way to turn as I locked up the wheels and slewed about in the most alarming manner. Bonnier must have thought that I was about to have a really good shunt, and from where I was sitting I would have agreed with him, for he braked much harder than necessary, obviously not wanting to get mixed up in my wreckage. I arrived at the right-hander fairly well out of control but, fortunately, the nose was pointing to the right and somehow we managed to scrape round. Those few extra yards gained on Jo were all I needed. Up through the gears along the last section I was determined not to lose an inch, nor to get overenthusiastic and make a mistake. Out of the last corner Jo was close, but not close enough. He came out of my slipstream and tried to come up on my right so, to give him his own back, I eased gently across to my right. But it made no difference, and I crossed the line with Jo's nose level with my back wheels. The time gap was, officially, 0·1 second, with Gurney 0·3 second behind.

The packed grandstands were obviously awaiting a German victory, for there was but a solitary cheer from the only Britisher there. And the poor chap with the flags was having the most awful time undoing his knot to haul down the German flag and replace the Union Jack. It was a close-run

thing. Colin Chapman was cock-a-hoop with delight, although perhaps his happiness was tinged with a certain amount of relief at getting his car back in one piece.

There have been, for me, many great races. There were two on Easter Monday, 1960, when I beat Stirling Moss in two 100-mile races at Goodwood. The first race was for Formula 2 cars of 1500 cc where Stirling had a Porsche and I had one of the first of the rear-engined Lotus machines. The main race of the day was for Formula 1 where again I had the new rear-engined 2·5-litre Lotus, while Stirling had his Cooper. It was very trying having the Master sitting inches away from my tail every inch of the way, for I knew that he was just waiting for the smallest error in my judgment to slip past and take the race. It was my first season in the Big League, and I think most people

73

thought I would drop a clanger somewhere along the line. But, if memory serves me right, I won from the Porsche by 4 seconds and from the Cooper by the more slender margin of 2 seconds.

The 1000-km race at the Nurburgring in 1964 was fun; I shared Ronnie Hoare's Ferrari with Graham Hill; our opposition being the works-entered cars from Maranello. By the time I took over from Graham, we were lying third and I managed to get up into first place before the fuel tank split, allowing petrol to spray all over the rear wheels. It was a memorable drive in a fabulous car, and for the first time I managed to cover more than two laps of the Nurburgring without either catching fire, breaking down, or having a shunt. Although we didn't finish, the memory of that race gives me a great deal of pleasure.

I suppose winning the American Grand Prix at Watkins Glen should give me the memory of a great race, but somehow it doesn't. Both Brabham and Moss were in front of me when their new V8 Climax engines blew up, but I did have to struggle with the rest of the pack, finally winning by only a few seconds. The memory of that race was spoiled for ever for it was the last race I drove for Team Lotus. I am, of course, proud of the fact that I became the first Scotsman ever to win a World Championship event, but somehow this seemed disconnected from the race itself.

Other cars, other races — they've all been great. The Project 214 Aston Martin at Le Mans, and the Tourist Trophy; the front-engined 3-litre Testa Rossa Ferrari I shared with Stirling at Sebring — we were leading comfortably when the stewards disqualified us for some technical infringement of the rules in the pits; the GTO Ferrari in which I won the 1962 Tourist Trophy by 2 seconds from Graham Hill in a similar car; the Lotus-Ferrari, built for me in America by Tom O'Connor and Jack Ross which put me on my back for three months when I wrote it off; even the 7-litre 600-hp Dodge I drove in the Daytona 500 in 1967 — my very last race — all 4000 lb of under-steering monster that it was... All these cars and the races were memorable in one way or another.

But the greatest race of all was the one which started, for me, some time about the middle of 1956 and finished in February 1967. It was all just great!

12

Denny Hulme

SOUTH AFRICAN GRAND PRIX 1972

I suppose the Monaco Grand Prix of 1967 must rank as my greatest race, because I know I drove well that day and, of course, it was my first GP win and the highlight of my world championship season. I was pretty pleased, too, with victory in the German Grand Prix later in the year, because to win at the Nurburgring just has to be the top achievement.

But for me there's another Grand Prix that means even more than these – the South African GP. And I don't mean just one GP, but a series of half a dozen, starting in 1967, when the Kyalami circuit was the venue for the first time.

If there's any race engraved on my heart it's this one. I've had a sort of love–hate relationship with the South African GP ever since I drove in it. It

Hulme's Yardley McLaren in the 1972 South African Grand Prix.

was a race I thought I could win on more than one occasion, and twice I thought I had, only to be hounded by mechanical problems. Over the six-year period from 1967 to 1972, I filled every place down to sixth ... and I didn't see the chequered flag until 1972!

When we went to Kyalami in 1967 I thought it was one of the nicest circuits in the world, and I immediately felt at home. Jack Brabham and I made up the front row on the grid with our Repco-powered Brabhams and without a doubt we had the fastest cars.

As the flag went down, I got a real flier of a start, and with a clear road ahead found it comparatively easy to build up a lead. I remember how good it felt, and prospects looked even better when Jack spun off on the third lap and I learned I had a 5-second lead.

From then on, I found it possible to extend the lead consistently. The car was running sweetly, the temperatures were showing good, and after 40 laps — half distance — I was a minute up on the second man. I told myself that all I had to do was to start slowing down and taking it steady.

I'd set a new record lap at the start of the race with almost full tanks, so I knew I had the race well under control. But I was keeping a close watch on tyre wear because we thought we might be pretty close to the bone. Fortunately, several cars were laying down oil, and this helped to reduce the rubber wear.

Then, around lap 60, I suddenly realised I was having to pump the brake pedal to get results. The next thing that happened was that I lost my brakes completely. I thought, 'No, this just can't be true,' and rushed into the pits to shout out that I would come in next time round for brake fluid. It was a dodgy moment coming in that second time without brakes and a lot of people had to jump smartly. The master cylinders were topped up and I went out again after losing 90 seconds, only to find I still hadn't any brakes. So I came in again and asked for the brakes to be bled, but this wasn't possible. I went out again and pressed on as well as I could, and finished fourth, 2 laps down to Pedro Rodriguez's Cooper-Maserati.

Looking back on it, I don't think I should have stopped, but at the time I thought it was only a matter of topping up with fluid and then making up the lost time. Without anchors, however, it just wasn't possible to motor quickly. Those remaining laps were a nightmare, trying to use the gearbox to slow down from over 160 mph down the straight and cornering gingerly because I had no means of braking if anything went wrong.

So one minute I thought I had my first GP win and nine championship points, and very soon I had only got three. Yes, it really was a big disappointment.

A year later I was less disappointed, even though I only finished fifth, because the BRM-engined McLaren I drove was not really a front-runner and we were up against two Lotuses and a Matra with Ford engines. My car was overweight,

and I estimated I was losing a whole second to Jim Clark's Lotus over the half mile from Club House Corner to the pits. I also had fuel starvation during the race, due to vaporisation, and for the last 28 laps the BRM engine showed zero oil pressure round most of the circuit. So, all in all, I was pretty satisfied with that fifth place.

For the 1969 race we had Ford power for our McLarens, and I felt much better to be on the front row of the grid with Jack Brabham and Jochen Rindt. Unfortunately I made a bad start, because I misjudged the drop of the flag, hesitated, and then got caught when the flag did fall. I also made a mess of the first corner at the end of the straight; everybody braked quicker than I anticipated, and I had to go round in a gear lower than I had used previously. Later on, I found that my car handled very badly on oil that had been dropped quite liberally on the track; I had to struggle really hard to keep everything under control and this prevented me from having a real go. An odd thing was that I finished the race with bare tyres on both left-hand wheels, whereas practice had suggested we would have plenty of rubber.

Anyway, there was no touching Jackie Stewart and his Matra that day and I just couldn't cope with Graham Hill's Lotus. But things were looking up, for this time I was third. Maybe I could improve on that in 1970?

Well, I did, coming second to Jack Brabham in what was to be my highest GP placing of the whole season. Jack was driving his new Brabham BT33, and was very impressive and I had a new McLaren M14A which also promised well. Both of us were on Goodyear tyres, and beforehand we had put in some useful tyre testing at Riverside. I am sure this gave us something of an advantage. I had a tougher problem than Jack, though, for while he started from the front row I was way down in the third line. Jackie Stewart was giving

the March 701 its first race airing, and he gave me some trouble for a while before I got past him just before half distance to take that second place.

So I'd now been to Kyalami four times, and my score was a fifth, fourth, third, and second. Surely it had to be first in 1971...

Things didn't look so hopeful after practice, because I was again on the third row of the grid with the new McLaren M19, and pole-man Jackie Stewart was 1·3 seconds quicker than I was. All the same, my car was handling well and I reckoned that if only I could get a good start then I'd be in business.

Jackie Stewart obliged by hesitating off the line, and so did Chris Amon with his Matra, so I took off after Clay Regazzoni's Ferrari and

Emerson Fittipaldi in his Lotus 72. My McLaren was working like a dream. After 4 laps I was past Fittipaldi and started to haul in Regazzoni. Eventually I got on to the Ferrari's tail, and the slip-stream tow meant that I was hitting the rev limiter (which was set at 10,200 rpm) so I switched it off and pressed on hoping that the engine would hold up. After 17 laps I pushed ahead of Regazzoni, which wasn't too difficult because the Ferrari wasn't handling too well.

So there I was, out in front, just like 1967, and the McLaren was working beautifully. Five laps to go and my pit signal told me I was a couple of seconds ahead of Mario Andretti's Ferrari. Mario had gradually got quicker as the Ferrari used up fuel — they had to start with far more gallons

Opposite: Hulme (no. 12) leading Fittipaldi, Hailwood, Cevert, and Peterson during the 1972 South African Grand Prix.

aboard because of the thirst of the 12-cylinder engines — but I was confident that I could hold him at bay. All I wanted was a few lucky breaks overtaking slower competitors, and perhaps a tow along the straight.

Then it happened. When I was going round Barbecue Corner I felt the McLaren wandering a little. My first thought was that I either had a puncture or one of the tyres was starting to get some build-up on it. I glanced round at all the wheels, but everything seemed okay. My next reaction was to try to stop worrying; I thought it was a case of those mental jitters you get when you're in the lead and hoping and praying that nothing will go wrong until the last lap is over.

I was wrong. As I went down into Sunset Corner and hit the brakes the car swerved across the track. I knew then I was in a heap of trouble. Mario caught me up and went rushing past into the lead. My right rear wheel was wobbling badly, and I just didn't know what was wrong. There was no time to find out at that stage, so I just hustled on as quickly as I could; everything was fine between 80 and 90 mph on a constant throttle, but under braking or acceleration the car was wandering all over the place.

I was determined to finish, and I did, but by then I had been passed by other competitors — I was even lapped by Andretti — and came home in sixth place. The trouble was caused through losing the bolt securing the upper radius arm. The Kyalami jinx had struck again! It really wasn't much consolation to read in the motoring magazines that I was the moral victor.

When I went to Kyalami in March of 1972 I hadn't scored a Grand Prix win since Mexico towards the end of 1969; but my McLaren had gone well to finish second in the Argentine GP in January, and somehow I thought I might do well under the South African sun.

Things didn't look too good during practice, because my car always seemed to be getting fitted with a new engine, and my new race engine only arrived just in time, the night before the GP. Then, on race morning, we found oil leaking from the back of the crankshaft and the mechanics only just managed to get it right before the warm-up.

This time I was on the second row of the grid, and I made one of the finest starts I remember. I got it all spot-on and gunned into the first corner ahead of everyone. I was still heading the bunch at the end of the first lap, but I knew it couldn't last, because Jackie Stewart was hammering up in his Tyrrell and from timing in practice we knew he was up to half a second quicker than us on the straight.

Sure enough, Jackie slipped by on the next lap, but I was able to keep Emerson Fittipaldi and Mike Hailwood just far enough behind to outdrag them on the straight. Things seemed to be settling down to a pattern, but then I noticed that the water temperature was beginning to soar after running the new 12-series Ford DFV hard at 10,500 rpm. It seemed better to be a little prudent, so after 17 laps I let Emerson and Mike through and ran comfortably in fourth spot.

'Mike the Bike' was in super form with his Surtees and, on lap 23, he picked off Fittipaldi and set off in chase of Jackie Stewart. Then, just when he looked like grabbing the lead, he had the mother and father of an incident when something failed in the rear suspension and he had to fight like mad to come to a halt relatively unscathed.

So that was one 'problem' solved. Then Jackie Stewart ran into trouble. For several laps I'd smelt hot oil, but didn't know where it was coming from; in fact, a bolt had come out of Jackie's gearbox and the lubricant was draining away. So after 44 laps, Emerson was in front and I was second, about 5 seconds behind.

79

Then I found it possible to close on Emerson. I think he was having some sort of handling trouble, but my Goodyear tyres were performing beautifully, and on lap 57 I slipped past him to take the lead. After that things went smoothly, and 3 laps later I cut my revs to 10,000, and later to 9500.

All I had to do was cruise through to lap 79, but as I went round Kyalami I couldn't help wondering whether history was about to repeat itself. After all, it had happened in 1967, and again in 1971...

But this time all went well, and I crossed the line 14·1 seconds ahead of Fittipaldi. After six years of trying and so nearly getting there in two races, I felt there was some justice in motor-racing after all!

81

13
Paul Frere

BELGIAN GRAND PRIX 1956

Possibly, many more of my races would be remembered by those interested in motor-racing if I had not happened to win Le Mans in 1960, co-driving with Olivier Gendebien. This seems to have drawn a blanket over most of the rest of my racing career, which practically came to an end with the victory in that most famous of all European races. Only those really in the game know, however, that the most glamorous victory does not necessarily crown the best personal performance. In fact, the choice I had to make to give an account of my best race lay between two in which I only finished second — the Eifel race at Nurburgring in an HWM in 1953, run in pouring rain, and the Belgian Grand Prix of 1956 also partly run in the rain — and one which I won under

a blazing hot sun, the South African Grand Prix of 1960. The reason I have chosen the Belgian Grand Prix is that its venue is so well known and because most of its actors are still well remembered by all enthusiasts who have grown out of their teens.

When I took up motor-racing — remember there was much less money in racing twenty years ago than today — I was quite determined that I would not race on a fully professional basis. Firstly, because I did not want to forsake my career as a motoring writer, which showed some promise; secondly, because I wanted racing always to be a pleasure, deciding for myself when and where I wanted to race, rather than having to dart from one venue to another to earn my living or honour a

contract. Moreover, I had always been fully aware of the risks of motor-racing and felt that it was ridiculous to accept them if the pleasure and satisfaction I got out of racing did not warrant them. This had been brought home to me rather forcibly when, practising for the Swedish Grand Prix of 1955 — a sports car race — my 3-litre Ferrari Monza left the road and overturned, throwing me out with, fortunately, no worse consequences than a broken knee which kept me out of racing for the rest of the season and gave me something to think about.

There was no question for me that I would be back at the wheel as soon as possible, but when 'Lofty' England, then Jaguar's Competitions Manager, offered me a place in the Jaguar team

83

for 1956, I decided that I would confine my sporting activities for that year to those events in which I would be driving officially for the British make. Admittedly, I had made an exception by driving a Ferrari in the Sports Car Race at Spa, earlier in the year, but I firmly intended to keep to my decision for the rest of the season and was adamant that, even should the opportunity present itself, I would not take part in any Formula One event, not even the Belgian Grand Prix. So, even though the year before I had come fourth in that race, driving a works Ferrari, I had not been in touch with either the Royal Automobile Club of Belgium, or with any manufacturer, in order to arrange a drive for that event.

Fate stepped in a week before the Grand Prix when Luigi Musso, racing in the Nurburgring 1000 Kilometre Race, broke his arm as the car turned over on top of him. Ferrari were relying on Mike Hawthorn to replace him but, owing to a misunderstanding, he subsequently appeared to be also booked by Maserati. Ferrari had consequently brought five cars, of which one was painted yellow and was to be placed at the disposal of the Equipe Nationale Belge, with André Pilette as driver; but they were still one driver short. For two whole days, I was bombarded with telephone calls from Eraldo Sculati, Ferrari's team manager, either directly or via third parties, trying to make me revoke my decision.

I remained unconvinced by any of the arguments, for I had no desire to take charge of a single-seater after the lapse of a year, and in particular before the Belgian public. Hoping, therefore, that a solution would be found without resorting to my services, I deliberately did not go to Francorchamps for the first practice, on the Thursday, and only arrived when the Friday practice period was starting, intending to get to work on my press report. Evidently, no alternative

arrangement for driving the fourth team car had been possible, for when, upon my arrival at Stavelot, I asked Engineer Amorotti who would be driving it after all, he replied that they were still hoping it would be me, since otherwise the car would not be able to start.

Even this news did not make me change my mind, and for more than an hour and a half I watched the cars going by in the rain. In the end, egged on by friends who were dumbfounded by my attitude, and sorely tempted by the sight of that magnificent single-seater, a direct descendant of the formidable Lancias of 1955, waiting forlornly in the rain for a driver to take it out, I went off to find Sculati. Race or no race, I was dying to try what was no doubt the finest Grand Prix car of the period. Practising was almost at an end when I asked to be allowed to try it out, on the strict understanding that I would thereby be under no obligation to drive it in the race. Of course Sculati agreed and, from the moment I took my place at the controls, there could be no more doubts, either for myself or anyone else, over my participation in the Grand Prix.

The following day's practice, nevertheless, justified my misgivings that I would be out of practice. I put in a dozen laps in all, without being able to get below 4 minutes 23 seconds, while Peter Collins, who had never been any faster than I when we were both driving HWM's some years before, had got down to around 4 minutes 15 seconds (which was still considerably longer than Fangio's almost incredible best practice lap of 4 minutes 9·5 seconds) achieved under ideal conditions on the first day. It was therefore obvious that my lack of practice was making itself felt, which in retrospect seems rather odd as only two weeks before I had been lapping the Reims circuit in a D-type Jaguar in times which were in the Mike Hawthorn bracket. Obviously, I did not

Frere in the Ferrari he only agreed to drive at the last minute.

feel really at ease, and I feared that I would put up a mediocre performance on the morrow, particularly as, of the 14 cars which would be competing, at least 10 would be driven by some of the best drivers in the world. The rest of the Ferrari team consisted of Fangio, Collins, and Castellotti, with André Pilette in a similar car painted yellow. The Maserati drivers were Moss, Behra, and Perdisa and, as private entries, Villoresi, Louis Rosier, and the Spanish driver Godia-Fales. Finally there were two very fast Vanwalls in the hands of Trintignant and Schell.

Our four team cars, and the one to be run by the Equipe Nationale, were all exactly alike. The only difference was that for the day of the race the Fangio and Collins cars had been fitted with a lower final gearing to give them more speed up the long rise of the back leg of the course. They were the cars which had been handed over to Ferrari by Lancia during the previous season, and had been modified in the light of the experience of the Maranello factory. The principal alteration was replacement of the side tanks by a large tank at the back. The framework which used to contain the fuel tanks had been retained and smoothed-in with the body; it still enclosed small tanks, of which one was used for a reserve supply. The rear suspension had likewise been modified and the front of the chassis strengthened. This work had put some 55 lb on to the weight of the vehicle, whose dry weight was now 1420 lb.

The front-mounted, Jano-designed V-8 engine,

85

Frere round a bend during the Belgian Grand Prix.

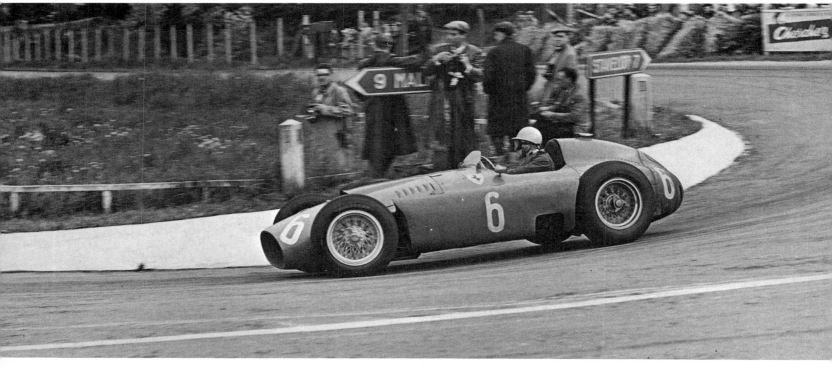

of Lancia origin, with four overhead camshafts and four double-choke Solex carburettors, had been further developed by Ferrari and, according to the figures shown to me by Engineer Amorotti, the best of the ones fitted to our cars delivered 272 bhp at 8200 rpm, and the least powerful 268 at the same engine speed, the slight drop in maximum power being made up for in the medium speed range. The gearbox had five speeds, of which first was used only for starting, and a stop came into action immediately second gear was engaged. This was a pity because, since the engine ran very irregularly below 4500 rpm, getting away in second gear from La Source hairpin was a difficult business. The brakes were magnificent and the steering was extraordinarily light

and reversible; so much so that at first I had the greatest difficulty in keeping the car straight. I think it must have been my lack of familiarity with this steering, which in itself was superb, which prevented me from getting closer to the practice times put up by my team-mates.

Whereas Saturday had been a brilliantly sunny day, Sunday started off ominously and, a few minutes before the start, rain began to fall. It continued to do so intermittently for two-thirds of the race, alternately wetting different parts of the course, while others were drying out. Moss was driving the fastest of the Maseratis, which had a more streamlined body with high sides coming over the driver's shoulders, and he took the lead, followed by Collins and Fangio. I found myself in a group of four cars, consisting of Behra's Maserati, the two Vanwalls, and my own Ferrari. Along the straights and getting away from the corners, the Vanwalls were the fastest, while the Maseratis appeared slightly inferior to the Ferraris in sheer maximum. On the other hand, the Italian cars appeared much more at ease in the corners than the two British vehicles but, every time we went round La Source hairpin, the Ferrari would lose several lengths because of its lack of power at low revolutions. Once he had passed Trintignant's Vanwall, Behra pulled away and soon afterwards Trintignant's car developed trouble.

That left me alone with Schell and our scrap lasted for several laps. Having managed to pass him after the rapid 'S'-bend at Masta, I remained in front of him until we got to La Source, where he passed me on acceleration, coming out of the slow corner. This went on for several laps until I arrived at La Source sufficiently ahead of my opponent to prevent him from making up his leeway before the climb after the pits. Once he had lost ground, Harry appeared to lose heart as well, and dropped back rapidly. I now continued on my own, gaining confidence as I got more used to the car, while the pits signalled to me that I was sixth, Fangio having in the meantime got the better of Moss. Hardly had I been informed of my position when I saw Moss running at full speed down the hill, having abandoned his Maserati, minus a rear wheel, at the side of the road. So that made me fifth!

Fifth? What am I saying? Soon my cousin, posted as usual at La Source, was indicating that I was fourth, as Castellotti had been forced to retire his Ferrari with transmission failure. Already fourth, my finishing position the previous year, and this was only the eleventh lap, hardly a third of the race run off! It seemed to me that I had not taken the wrong decision after all in agreeing to drive. If only the car would last! Without seeing anyone either in front or behind me, I continued to do my best while taking into account the treacherous surface of the course as, with the rain coming down in showers, one found that a spot which had been dry on the preceding lap was now wet and slippery while others were drying up. It soon became evident that I was finding my form again, for the pits signalled Behra's diminishing lead; 26 seconds, 23 seconds, 20 seconds, 18 seconds, and soon, on the back leg from Stavelot to La Source, I saw the red Maserati in the distance. I now realised that third place was within my reach and any remaining impression of lack of practice disappeared. The 15 laps which I had done had helped to restore my confidence completely and, at the wheel of the Ferrari, I felt as if I had done nothing else in my life but lap the Francorchamps circuit at around 120 mph — remember that was in 1956 and the back leg was much slower and narrower than it is today.

Then, when I had got to within 100 yards of the Maserati, what should I see but Fangio's Ferrari by the roadside, just after Stavelot! After a momentary consternation, I realised that I was now actually fighting for second place! Redoubling my efforts, I succeeded in taking Behra coming out of the fast Burnenville curve, just before Malmedy bend. Passing him at this spot caused me considerable amusement for, on the eve of the race, I had argued with him about the best way to take that bend, and in particular, where to start braking for it. According to him, he kept flat-out down the slope as far as the Bridge — still there today — before touching his brakes. Having always braked at least 80 yards earlier, and considering this to be about the limit, I had been considerably impressed by his description but utterly unable to imitate it. During the race, however, it was in that particular bend that I was able to catch him up most, and where I finally passed him. Some racing-driver friends had already warned me that to do oneself what other drivers said they did on the course would be sheer suicide. At that period of the race I did not doubt that wise advice for one moment!

I pressed on for another 2 laps, trying to consolidate my advantage over Behra and, the course now being almost completely dry, I went round first in 4 minutes 18 seconds and then in 4 minutes 17·5 seconds. By now I had regained about 30 seconds of the 2-minute lead which Collins, henceforth the undisputed leader, had built up over me in the first half of the 310-mile race. My best lap was the third fastest that day, Fangio having taken 4 minutes 17·4 seconds on his eleventh lap, when the course was still wet in places, while Moss, who had taken over Perdisa's car, had achieved a lap in 4 minutes 14·7 seconds in his efforts to get into third place.

Provided the car went on to finish my second place was assured for Behra's Maserati, which had already lost third gear, now developed engine trouble as well, and so I drew away by a whole lap from poor Jeannot, who crept round to the finish and then had to push his car over the line as soon as the winner had crossed it, to finish sixth behind Moss, Schell, and Villoresi, who had all passed him by then.

Both for Collins and for myself this was probably the greatest day to date of our careers as racing drivers. He had won, for the first time, a major event counting towards the World Championship, while I, by finishing second, had achieved a success which I do not believe has been equalled by an amateur driver in modern Grand Prix racing; even today this is still the best placing achieved by a Belgian driver in his national Grand Prix.

What a pity that John Heath, who had been killed the previous year in the Mille Miglia, could not have been there to see, coming into the first three places, Collins, Frere, and Moss — three drivers who had matured in his team of HWMs!

14
Olivier Gendebien

MILLE MIGLIA
1956

Anger can win you a race. This I discovered in 1956 — my first full season with the World Champion Ferrari Works Team — when the team manager told me it was up to me to defend the Ferrari colours in a commercial saloon on the extraordinary Mille Miglia circuit.

I suppose it was my easy success in the Grand Touring category of the Tour de Sicile which made him choose me to drive the Ferrari 250 GT saloon. Also in 1955 I came very near to taking victory from a Mercedes in this class. Ferrari himself was particularly keen, we all knew, to make sure of winning against the successful German firm. One thing fans tend to forget in the excitement of watching motor-racing is that it is the commercial classes which do most to sell motor-cars.

Recollecting the Tour de Sicile, however, I was a little reluctant to take on driving in the Grand Touring Class Ferrari Saloon. For in that race I had been soaked to the skin driving through rainstorms in what was supposed to be a saloon! So I felt quite justified in insisting that this time the workshop ensured that my car was watertight. 'That's okay, Olivier,' they told me. 'Don't worry about a thing. The car will be perfect.' So I relaxed and waited for the night start of the Mille Miglia.

We, my navigator Jacques Washer and I, were making the night start because our car was not one of the fastest. The rest of the Ferrari team — Castelotti, Collins, Fangio, and Musso — were to make their starts at intervals through the rest of the following morning as they entered the hectic battle which is the Mille Miglia.

Not only was it night, however. After only a few kilometres it began to rain. It didn't take me thirty seconds to realise that we had no windscreen to speak of, and that there had in fact been nothing done to make the car watertight. At that point I did not yet know that we were to drive through almost 1000 kilometres of rain, but already my anger was rising; an anger which really changed my whole attitude towards my car; I now drove with a total lack of my habitual respect for machines, a respect equal to that which I had learnt to have for horses. I pushed the car to its limits, almost beyond, braking suddenly or brutally crashing the gears. In short, I was harsh and imprudent, and would not have to wait long before paying the price . . .

Anger had in fact put me in a position of strength and utter determination to win in spite of the disadvantages. And because I covered literally hundreds of miles in this dangerous ill-humour there were incidents — to use a very mild term — which probably would not have happened if my car had been perfectly prepared.

One of these occurred on a long straight stretch of road alongside the Adriatic a little before we reached Pescara. There are many moments in motor-racing when you have to take calculated risks. These nearly always involve only yourself, your own safety and, of course, your navigator who should know that his life is likely to be in as much danger as yours. But in the 1956 Mille Miglia there was a rare moment of understanding between me and a spectator. A spectator? Well, he was a railway guard who happened to be performing his duties at a time when they conflicted with my intentions! From a considerable distance I saw a raised barrier across the road. We were travelling at our maximum speed — about 240 km/h — and had already decided not to slow down, when I saw the barrier descending 'Out of the question. Impossible! I just won't stop!' That was what I thought to myself as I continued to bear down on the barrier, flashing my

lights and hooting. Although it was broad daylight I wanted to be sure I was seen and understood. And indeed the guard appeared to have grasped the situation. I have tried often, since then, to imagine what must have passed through his mind. At that moment, however, I saw only one, or rather two things: the first being the barrier, which had come to rest about 5 feet from the ground, as I passed through; the second was on glancing to the left — I could see the express scarcely a few yards away. Such was the risk and generosity of the guard, but what a tremendous responsibility! I wanted to stop, to thank him, to embrace him, to smother him in gifts; but as I very well knew it was out of the question. Our paths had crossed. There had been a momentary battle of wills. A moment of drama had passed and as it did so I realised again that my will had been sharpened by anger and that skill and timing and judgment had all operated perfectly in this mood.

Perhaps it was pure luck? I did not consider it any further for ahead of me lay the road with more problems and, as it turned out, dangerous dramas which tested even the iron nerve of Jacques Washer.

It had started to rain again. My handkerchiefs were soaked, and Jacques had to sacrifice his shirt in an attempt to keep the windscreen relatively dry, at the same time keeping an eye on his maps — and we were nearing the mountain. I had my foot down and approached a banked corner at too great a speed: the car turned a complete circle and its side hit a large pile of gravel. The collision was so violent that I immediately thought of the possibility of fire: fire — that's my obsession. I shouted to Jacques, 'Let's get out!' But the doors were jammed tight and we had to force them open with our feet — luckily it was a lightweight aluminium body. I was already thinking 'That's the end of that race', but surprisingly

Gendebien driving through heavy rain during the
1956 Mille Miglia.

the car was not too badly damaged, except the doors which Washer managed to hold closed with all the ties, belts, and pieces of string he could lay his hands on. In this elegant machine we managed to catch up with Costzetti, driving a Ferrari Sports, just before Florence; and I placed myself squarely in his tracks. I was hellbound; Jacques' face was pale and drawn and he did not utter a word — what good would it have done anyway? I couldn't hear a thing above the abominable clanking noises of the Ferrari. On the road from Bologna to Parma I saw Washer's fist hit the dashboard, almost as if to say 'Slow down!'; and there just ahead of us sped a small Stanguellini, half hidden by the spray of water thrown up in his wake — I just managed to miss him. But that is not all: what with this crazy machine and the slippery roads, with visibility almost nil — I spun around and around, eight times in all. If I may say so, practice makes perfect, and I almost arrived at the point where I could direct and then neutralise the spin.

Later at the Bologna checkpoint, among a group of mechanics, I saw the tall figure of Ferrari. He approached us, as we were still sitting in the car, trapped by the string-tied doors. I was transfixed with rage, incapable of uttering a single word. He said simply and calmly: 'You have five minutes' lead on Reiss.' He was referring to a German driving a Mercedes 300 SL. 'You must keep it until Brescia.'

There was nothing extraordinary in his words, but they were spoken in a profound, grave voice, charged with — how shall I say? — a certain weight, and upheld by a look that was so imperious as to make them resound as an order; an absolute necessity, making discussion superfluous. I have reservations concerning certain aspects of Ferrari's personality, but his 'presence' could not be denied, nor the effect of that presence on me.

No doubt Ferrari's success depended very largely on this ability to make his drivers grit their teeth and say, 'I'll show him!' Thus, once again in a mood of controlled anger, I set off again, foot hard down and absolutely determined to wring every last drop of speed out of the battle-scarred Ferrari. And thus, still fuming, I found myself at Brescia . . . at the head of the Grand Touring category, ahead of five factory-produced Mercedes 300 SL. In the overall classifications, I was fifth, lying behind Castelotti, Collins, Musso, and Fangio, all of whom were driving more powerful Ferraris than I. Exhausted and staggering I forgot my anger and was happy; I do believe that Ferrari was also, although he was always impenetrable and sparing with his compliments. In fact, that Mille Miglia of 1956 marked the beginning of the grand era of the Berlinette Ferrari 250 GT — a car which swept the board at so many later races.

15
Roy Salvadori

COPPA INTER-EUROPA 1963

The greatest car, the greatest circuit, and the greatest race have never coincided for me in a long career at the wheels of fast cars. There have been races in which I was proud of my performance, cars I have respected, and circuits which test a driver's skill and yet have an atmosphere which can be enjoyed. Perhaps, since I can't honestly say that one race stands high above others in my experience, I may be allowed to reminisce about some of the cars, circuits, and races. My first professional drive was with Bobby Baird, a motor-sport enthusiast from Belfast, who asked me to drive his 2·7-litre Ferrari at the Goodwood nine-hour event. This event taught me that longer stints at the wheel are preferable to the brief sessions of the Le Mans-type race, where fatigue

94

is due more to lack of sleep than the time spent at the wheel.

Baird and I shared a Ferrari in the Nine Hours — the first one to be held — and he found that he just could not manage to get to grips with the circuit. It wasn't his day. I was quite prepared to go the whole race on my own, but the regulations stated that drivers must change every two hours. So I drove for the stipulated period and came into the pits, where I handed over to Bobby. Then he took the Ferrari out for one lap and handed back to me.

We were in the lead but at dusk I was called in by one of the marshals who had noticed a sidelight failure, a delay that dropped us back in the queue for the flag. We eventually finished third. I found that I was as fresh at the end of that event as when the cars left the grid, and have seen no merit in the Le Mans musical-chair system since.

Aston Martin took notice of me after that event at Goodwood and in 1953 my long friendship with them began. I stayed with the incomparable

95

Feltham stable almost continuously until 1963. They were such pleasant people to work with, and the management of the team was meticulous. Car preparation was first-class and drivers were cushioned against run-of-the-mill worries from the time they set out for an event to the moment they arrived back home.

Aston Martin made only one error of judgment — their Formula 1 car. Its brief appearance on the racing scene prompted many to believe that the car was not up to the usual high standard of the products of the Feltham stable, but its only fault was that it was produced too late. There was nothing wrong with the car itself, in fact its first appearance was a copy-book example of what all racing-car manufacturers would like to see. They all dream of putting a new car on the grid for the first time and collecting the honours in the face of the rest of the world's tried and tested vehicles.

In May 1959, after a period of quiet development with the minimum publicity, two single-seater cars appeared at Silverstone for practice. Carroll Shelby drove one and I had the other.

My car was so well prepared and so perfect to handle that it took me just two laps on the first day and half a dozen on the second to establish my position on the front row of the grid with Moss, Brooks, and Brabham.

The race itself was all we could have wished. At the start I settled into third place and motored very quickly round the circuit without strain, holding that position until the Moss BRM fell out with a fractured brake pipe. Jack Brabham continued to circulate in his own tearaway style — this was to be his first championship year — and I contentedly followed in second place to the end of the race. During this time I noticed the fastest lap at a speed which equall the lap record for Formula 1 cars.

I was satisfied with my own performance that

day, and for a first showing of David Brown's new car the results were far better than had been expected. Peter Garnier of the *Autocar*, an expert not noted for over-enthusiastic praise, said in his sports page: 'Certainly within my memory no British car has had such an impressive first outing. Its performance was equal to that of any of the other current contenders on this circuit, and better than some of the well-established ones. I would go as far as to say, from the observations that were possible during the race, that in road-holding it is superior to any of them.'

It was such a pity that the car was brought out just eighteen months too late. It was a fine car, but having lagged behind in development it just could not catch up. This was the initial period of the lightweight, rear-engined Cooper and Lotus. With their greater power-to-weight ratio and better road-holding the 1959 and 1960 seasons saw them sweep the board and change the face of the sport. It was a tragedy for Aston Martin: if they had been able to race against cars of a similar design — Maseratis, Ferraris, and BRMs — they would have made a far deeper mark in Formula 1 racing. In August 1960 David Brown announced officially that his Formula 1 cars would not take part in any further events. It was the sad end of a great vehicle and the beginning of a new era of miniature racing . . . There is no doubt in my mind that the finest sports car ever produced in the 1950s was also a product of the David Brown group — the Aston Martin DBRI. For three years in succession it won the Nurburgring 1000 kilometres, considered by some to be the toughest race in the world.

I drove for Aston Martin in countless events — I've no idea how many — but I clearly remember my proudest moment in one of their cars at Monza. I had been told by Mr John Wyer, of Aston Martin-Lagonda, that they were pulling out of the

competitive field (at least for the time being). Their last race, he said, could well be the Coppa Inter-Europa, held before the Italian Grand Prix on Sunday, 8 September 1963.

Ferraris dominated the grid with eight 250 GTOs and there were a couple of E-type Jaguars to liven things up. Lucien Bianchi and I drove DB4 GTs.

For most of the first half of the three-hour event I had been hounding the red Ferrari of Mike Parkes. Then he pulled into the pits for fuel, and rejoined the race over a minute behind me. A few minutes later I was running dry and dived into the Aston pit where the mechanics were waiting on their toes. The lads moved like lightning and had

topped me up and sent me back on to the track 3 seconds before Mike came round again.

For the last 90 minutes of the race the duel between Mike and myself was carried on with tremendous intensity. For lap after lap just tenths of a second separated us, and the excited Italian spectators must have thought we were taking it in turns by arrangement to lead past the pits. At this stage I undoubtedly had the crowd on my side, as it had been announced over the loudspeaker system that Salvadori was really an Italian driving a British car. Later, when this information was corrected, my popularity with the crowd waned!

Sometimes in exciting races of this kind, where manufacturers' reputations are concerned, the

Salvadori leading at Oulton Park, 1957.

only people who know the truth of what's going on are the drivers. Only they know how hard they are trying and only they know the relative merits of the cars they are driving. Mike showed me more about Monza than I knew existed and in doing so helped me enormously to win the race. To follow him up to his braking points and through the tremendously fast corners of Monza was a revelation. Because I had slightly more maximum speed I was able to pass him on the straights, but he would always slipstream me and then out-accelerate me at the exit from the slow corner which led to the finish. And I realised that if Mike was within striking distance of me on the last lap he would win on his superior acceleration.

During the last few laps of the race I took the lead again and drove the Aston almost into the ground to try and lose the Ferrari, but still Mike hung on. Then, just two laps from the end, on the Lesmo Corner where Mike was outstandingly fast, we lapped some slower cars and what I had hoped for over the last 90 minutes happened — he was put off his line slightly and failed to get out of the corner quickly enough to slipstream me. From then on his race against me was over.

It was a good moment. David Brown had realised one of his dearest ambitions, to beat the near-invincible Ferraris on their home ground; we had pulled off a fine win in the marque's last event, and I had broken the GT lap record time and time again during the race. A satisfactory finale to my long and pleasant association with Aston Martin . . .

The Cooper Monaco, the other sports car in which I have spent a considerable time, is a completely different machine. Its smaller size, of course, has much to do with its dissimilar characteristics, as does the aft position of the power unit. Like all rear-engined cars it has the minimum breakaway and describes a very correct and cal-

culated line through a bend. Although I prefer a front-engined vehicle (maybe I'm just old-fashioned), there is no doubt that the rear-engined car cures many of the linkage troubles that were so frequently apparent in the older layouts, and the driver can be seated in an aerodynamically better position. Combined with the permitted lower frontal area of the car I suppose it was inevitable that this trend would eventually swamp the sport. But like an old salt hankering after sail, I wish we had those big bonnets in front of us again.

For reliability today I would still choose a Cooper Monaco. It is a more robust car than most; so often when I have seen a car break up, or lose a wheel, or fling off a bit of essential equipment, I have thanked heaven I was in a Cooper. Road-holding was excellent, though possibly not the best in the sports-car field; design was satisfactory, though not the ultimate, and there was unity and strength in the construction layout. This only goes to prove that the orthodox way of thinking has paid off in safe and steady successes over the seasons. The integrity of designer and constructor shows through . . .

Every driver has his favourite circuits, the places where he starts off with a twin advantage of superior knowledge and the confidence that it engenders. From my earliest days of competitive driving, Goodwood, Crystal Palace, and Silverstone have been my backyards. I have learned every mark on their surfaces, plotted every road repair and noted the scar it has left, watched every plant grow into a bush, and the bushes sprout into trees. I know each small undulation — and what it will do to a car. The cambers, rises, curves, and bends; after so many years I know them all like the lines on my face; in fact they put many of those lines there.

Strap yourself into the passenger seat of a light-weight E-type Jaguar with a five-speed gearbox and spend 1 minute 28·6 seconds with me on the circuit at Goodwood at competitive speed. Around once slowly, then past the pits in a flying start . . .

We run out of the chicane and ease over to the middle of the road, hitting the start-line in third gear at 5850 rpm (96 mph). At the line I change up to fourth gear, and to fifth on the outside of the track just 50 yards before the start of the sweep into Madgwick. Down to fourth again, aiming the car at the marshals' box on the inside of the curve. Through the long two-part bend with the back breaking away and the car aiming at the apex, then pointing towards the outside edge as we power into the next short straight. Holding fourth we line up after Madgwick, the car leaving the bend at 5500 rpm (112 mph).

Over on to the left side of the road, moving towards Fordwater, up into fifth. Fordwater is one of the nastiest bends, one that can be taken flat-out in the E-type, but a section that needs real driving to maintain the correct line. On the ill-defined apex – the curve is long and irregular – a small crossed marker indicates the point at which the radiator should be aimed. Aim it, and the car will move over to the right. It feels rather late, but if we turn in too soon on this bend the line of the car is completely wrong. At the apex the car is still in fifth travelling at 5500 rpm (134 mph) and will become wildly uncomfortable if the back starts to break away, a manoeuvre to be avoided at all costs.

The exit from Fordwater – which seems to go on and on – is a wicked piece of road, rough and oddly sloped. The car must be allowed to follow the dictates of the road and permitted to flip over to the outside of the track.

Up a small rise and down into fourth gear for the right-hand curve before St Mary's. We take the right-hand curve tightly in to the marker, tucking in well and preventing the car from breaking

away too much. If we're not well up against the right-hand side of the track here it will be extremely difficult to negotiate the left-hand part of the bend which immediately follows.

Down the slight dip into the left-hander and through with tremendous thrust, keeping a tight control of the car over a bad opposite camber. Out of St Mary's in fourth at 4950 rpm (100 mph) and line up for Lavant, running over to the centre and then to the right of the track as the car completes its exit from St Mary's.

The approach to Lavant is taken from the left-hand side of the road, and just before the braking point for the corner we record 5650 rpm in fourth gear (114 mph). Lavant – the first part – must be taken tightly, whamming the car around and breaking the back out, hugging the inside all the time. Between the two apexes of Lavant we let the Jaguar out into the middle of the road and bring it back in for the second apex, though not quite so violently as for the first.

Cut over to the left coming out of Lavant, hitting the straight at 5350 rpm in fourth (108 mph), letting the car have its head and using the minimum amount of steering. If the car is steered too deliberately here the tyres will cut into the road, reducing our speed.

Up to fifth for the kink on Lavant Straight, diving towards Woodcote at 6100 rpm (148 mph) on the fastest section of the course.

Woodcote, the long sweeping bend before the chicane, should be entered late and from the extreme left-hand side of the road. The car is in third by the time it uses the first part of the curve and is in the middle of the track. Swinging over to the right the late apex is taken smoothly and the car allowed to go over to the left once more before the chicane itself.

The chicane is wider – and quicker – than most people imagine. From the left-hand side of the

road the car is brought over to the right and the low guard wall is passed within about a foot. The chicane wall on the left is clipped — how closely depends on the degree of one's judgment — and the car sweeps out at about 50 mph in third, picking up to over 70 by the time the obstacle is left behind. And so on to another lap.

For me Goodwood was not the most magnificent circuit in Britain, nor even the most interesting. Oulton Park beat it for variety and beauty, Aintree and Silverstone for size. But to me Goodwood has always had an atmosphere second to none. Perhaps it is because of its association

with summer, with green grass and horses, with amateur sport rather than commerce, with the air of moneyed leisure. Or perhaps it is the memory of the motoring Goodwood of the past, of Reg Parnell in the early fifties, of Fangio in the 16-cylinder BRM, of Hawthorn and Collins in their red Ferraris, of the great Moss starting his career in the HWM, of the colour and excitement of the days when I was piling up my own experience. Whatever the reasons, give me the recollection of a car and a competition at Goodwood on an English summer's day and you can keep the rest of the world!

101

16
Graham Hill

MONACO GRAND PRIX 1965

The 1965 Monte Carlo was a race which I have always considered to be one of the best races I have ever run or ever won. I did reasonably well in practice — I put up the fastest time and therefore, as I had won the race the two previous years, I was considered the favourite for the race that year. Now that is something I never really like to be — because everyone expects an awful lot of the favourite and it certainly raises the tension.

Monte Carlo is always a tricky race, one of the trickiest circuits in the world, because it is so easy to be just a little bit untidy at any one particular corner, clobber a kerb with the wheel and break the suspension or break a wheel or cause yourself to spin off. And, of course, there is just nowhere to spin at Monte Carlo; you bounce off hotels, night-

102

clubs, brick walls, telegraph poles, street lamps. Everything around is absolutely solid, although we have managed to get a few Armco barriers set up at one or two spots which might prevent us from coming to a stop rather smartly.

It's a proper road circuit and one of the few remaining in the world. You can look at pictures of the first race track — I think it was 1929, the year I was born — and the track looks exactly the same. The only difference is the cars; they are a bit antique-looking. The circuit hasn't altered its shape at all, although the chicane has been moved in the last year to make it just a little bit safer. In fact, if the chicane had been in the right place — in the place where it is now — I wouldn't have been forced to go up an escape road

taking avoiding action during the race in 1965.

The race had been on for about 25 laps and I was in the lead when I came over the brow of a hill towards the chicane. I was doing about 120 mph at that particular point and was just getting on the brakes as I started to go down the hill. As I straightened up and the chicane came into view, I saw Bob Anderson in his Brabham literally creeping down towards the chicane — apparently the car was stuck in first gear. I had seen no flag and no signals or anything. All I could see as I blasted over the hill — in that fleeting second that you get to make a decision — was that he was going to be occupying the chicane at about the time that I wanted to flash through it doing about 95 mph.

There was only one thing to do: I just stood on

103

Hill during the Monaco
Grand Prix.

the brakes as hard as I could, locking them up. I made as if to go through the chicane and I left things until the point of no return, and then I saw that there was just no way I could get through without clobbering him. I came off the brakes for a second so that I could steer and changed direction down the escape road. Then I stood on them again and I left some rare old skid marks. I came to a grinding halt well up the escape road. I had to get out of the car, push it backwards on to the track, climb in, and then start the engine. Well, of course, all this took time and by then the leaders had gone through. I had lost I don't know how many seconds: about 35. And I had had quite a comfortable lead. Anyway, I lost over half a minute in this operation which dropped me right back to fifth place. I was pretty narked about this — it had more or less knocked me out of the fight for the lead. So I jumped into the car and set off in hot pursuit.

The race was 100 laps and I had done 25 so I still had three-quarters of the race to make up the time. I was a bit cheesed off over the whole business — if I had come by a second later I would have been able to squeeze through, but as it was I just couldn't get down to a sufficiently slow pace to follow Anderson through the chicane at his speed. It was bad luck that he just happened to be in that position. There was nothing he could have done about it — he was stuck in first gear. There should really have been a warning — the yellow flag should have been hung out warning the drivers that there was a car proceeding at a slow pace ahead. I would have lifted off a bit earlier and approached the brow of the hill a bit slower; then I would have been able to stop.

Things have been tightened up since then and I don't think the same thing could happen again. In any case, the chicane has now been moved 100 yards farther on down the quayside which means there is more room to brake and a car could, in fact, get stopped before the chicane. If there was a pile-up and the chicane got blocked now, anyone coming round the brow of the hill would have time to stop. This place had, of course, been the scene of a famous crash in 1957 involving Moss, Hawthorn, and Collins; Fangio managed to slip through the debris. Nobody wants a race to get messed up because of something stupid like that. Anyway, I set off after the leaders and gradually whittled the time down.

First, I caught up my team-mate Stewart, who had moved into first place when I went down the escape road, but Stewart had spun at Ste Devote and lost the lead on lap 30. I caught him up and passed him; I set off to catch up Surtees and Bandini who were both driving for Ferrari. They were having a tremendous ding-dong among themselves. Brabham had been after them and had taken the lead on lap 34, but on lap 43 he ran out of oil and had to coast into the pits to retire. I was having a terrific scrap and broke the lap record a number of times — I was motoring faster and faster as the fuel load got lighter. Gradually I got to see this tussle going on and then, of course, the Ferrari team saw that I was closing up. They made frantic efforts to signal to their drivers to stop dicing for the lead and go faster. As soon as Bandini and Surtees got the message from their pit signals that I was catching them up, they started to pull the stops out. By the time I actually caught them up, Bandini had got a bit clear. On lap 53 I got by Surtees and set off after Bandini. I had quite a few goes at passing him.

Monte Carlo is an extremely difficult place to overtake anybody and you've really got to work at it. You start building up to pass somebody more or less a lap in advance. If you decide that the best place to take him is at the Gasworks corner, you've got to start the manoeuvre more or less from the Gasworks on the preceding lap so that you arrive at the Tobacconist's corner – the one before the Gasworks – in just the right position to make a 100 per cent job of taking the corner on the limit, and that little bit quicker, to draw alongside him going down the straight – and hoping to pass him under braking for the Gasworks corner.

It takes a lot of planning, a lot of strategy, to actually pass somebody; it just doesn't occur in a flash if the bloke's going at roughly the same speed as yourself. You don't simply say to yourself, 'Right, I'll pass him now'; you must build up for it. You probe and you feel; all the time that you are racing against him you are working out where you are going to pass him, where is going to be the best place to pass, where he is a little bit quicker than you and where you are a little bit quicker than he. All these things have to be weighed up and you've just got to time it right. It takes a lot of working out – unless the fellow makes a mistake; then, of course, you want to be in the right spot when he makes the mistake. If you pressure somebody hard enough he might make a mistake, but then you have still got to be on his tail and in control to take advantage of it. And this is not always possible.

You haven't just got to make up a car's length; if you're right up on his tail – nose to exhaust pipe – you have to make up three cars' lengths to get ahead and allow yourself room to cut in again – which is a lot when it is a tight circuit. You have to follow the leader round the Gasworks turn and round the Station hairpin, so there are very few places to pass. One of the best places for overtaking is after the Gasworks, and it's the safest, but it requires making a much quicker exit and being sufficiently closed up to be able to pass under acceleration before Ste Devote.

In the end I got Bandini at the same place as I got Surtees – on the short straight going down the

hill towards Mirabeau after leaving the Casino Square. It's a very short sharp downhill stretch and I managed to come round Casino Square just that little bit better, holding a tighter line, and I got down the inside of both of them under braking.

Bandini gave me quite a hard time but eventually I got by him; he didn't give in, though, and we had a rare old ding-dong. Then Surtees got by Bandini and put the pressure on me for a while around the 80th lap and I know I put in some very fast laps at about this time. It was a tremendous race and I think that this, with the 1962 German Grand Prix, were probably my best races ever. They both had some extraordinary circumstances. (I had had a collision with a cine-camera in practice at Nurburgring.) To have actually won the race at Monte Carlo after having had to push the car back on to the track and then push-start it was quite something. The added pleasure that really put the icing on the cake was the fact it was my hat-trick; it gave me three wins in three consecutive years, which made it even more satisfying and memorable for me.

Surtees was really very unlucky – after an extremely good fight, he had the disappointment of running out of fuel on the last lap and, though he was classified as a finisher in fourth place but one lap behind, it was tragic that he was not able to take second place. Nothing is more galling than to run out of fuel on the last lap; it does make you think that the whole 99 previous laps have been a complete waste of time. When you have really been fighting tooth and nail, to have that sort of thing happen is a very bitter pill indeed. Two hours, 37 minutes, 39·6 seconds is a long time to be motoring flat-out on a circuit like Monte Carlo.

My car had run perfectly; I had absolutely no trouble with it – my hat-trick was a great credit to BRM and a tremendous technical achievement,

Hill leads Stewart, Bandini, and Brabham at
Monte Carlo in 1965.

Graham Hill in his BRM rounding a bend during
the Monaco Grand Prix.

because Monte Carlo is undoubtedly one of the toughest circuits on a car.

The prize-giving itself is a very proper and pukka affair at the Hotel de Paris, which is one of the swankiest hotels in the world, and a very swept-up do. I always somehow managed to forget to take my dinner jacket and arrived wearing a lounge suit; for three years I have arrived in an ordinary suit and everyone else was wearing a dinner jacket. The trouble is, I have noticed since, that when I have taken my dinner jacket I haven't won the race, so I don't like to anticipate the victory banquet in this way. Immediately after the race Prince Rainier and Princess Grace received me up on the dais and, of course, they were getting quite used to seeing me; there were a few 'Not again!' sort of remarks. They always attend the race and present the awards, and show a lot of interest in the event.

On the night of the race we went to the Tip-Top, a little bar which doesn't seem to have much to recommend it except that it sells drink, but it is a popular meeting place for all the British contingent — we always go there. I look in every year and every year the owner treats me to a drink — this time it was champagne. After the official prize-giving I had my drink and a plate of spaghetti with the owner of the Tip-Top. By this time it was three or four o'clock in the morning and I was starving again: after 100 laps around Monte Carlo it was not very surprising.

I remember Betty and I spent the next day on the beach at Cap Ferrat and I really felt completely relaxed, though that's hardly the word. I knew that I had taken a lot out of myself mentally and physically, but the victory had really put a glow in me. I don't think I have ever felt quite like it before. A tremendous feeling of peace, serenity, and fulfilment. I just felt entirely relaxed and every muscle in my body felt as if it was completely rested.

17
Baron de Graffenried

BRITISH
GRAND
PRIX
1949

The first British motor race to be dignified with the title 'Grand Prix' was held at Silverstone on a sunny May afternoon in 1949. Ideally I suppose it should have been won by one of the many famous British drivers in the race. But national prestige and luck do not always go hand in hand, even for a motor-racing nation as great as Britain. Perhaps winning the World Cup for soccer may have had something to do with the venue of the match in Britain? I do not know; but I feel that with motor-racing the spectators have little importance. The driver's battle is a lonely one. He drives to victory or death in a tin cocoon, unable to hear the spectators for the roar of his engine. The victors on that bright day in 1949 were Italy and Switzerland.

De Graffenried in the 1949 British Grand Prix.

Back in 1949 Grand Prix motor-racing was much tougher on the drivers than it is now. For instance, when we were heading for a circuit I frequently drove the lorry which carried our two racing cars so that our mechanics could rest and sleep. This was a task which all racing drivers undertook willingly because the mechanics often had to stay awake all night preparing a car for a race after practice. It could take the whole night to change a back axle and, since they broke very easily, cylinder blocks had to be replaced regularly.

Driving towards Silverstone on the Thursday before the race, we got lost in the English countryside on winding English roads. My navigation was not helped by the fact that I was concentrating on

driving on the 'wrong' side of the road! However, we eventually found a very pleasant place called the Cornhill Hotel near Towcester and only a short drive from the Silverstone circuit. Apart from being an agreeable hotel it had the additional merit of providing space for greasy mechanics to work on our Maseratis.

We were a small private team and called ourselves Scuderia Enrico Platé. The two drivers were Prince Bira and me. Bira and I were great friends which is an essential state of affairs for drivers in a small team. We trusted one another but more than that we trusted Enrico Platé who had a particular genius for preparing Maseratis. On the Friday morning of the trials Bira and I were more than happy with the 1500-cc two-stage

De Graffenried leads Chiron at Silverstone, 1949.

supercharged Maseratis he handed over to us for the practice spells before this first British Grand Prix.

In fact we had every reason to be pleased with the cars. Although the practice sessions were fairly short the cars felt very good, we both agreed. And, more to the point, we both earned ourselves places on the front row of the starting grid by achieving fast practice laps. Alongside us the following afternoon would be Villoresi in a low-chassis version of the 4CLT/48 Maserati which Bira and I were driving. Villoresi had clocked the fastest practice lap time of 83·2 mph. Bira ran him a close second at 82·95 mph and Peter Walker in his 1935 ERA was third fastest at 81·08 mph. My own best speed was 80·83 round the 3-mile circuit. The last of the front-row drivers was Bob Gerard in his 1937 ERA B/C with the Jameson supercharger. Bob's fastest lap time was a mere second slower than mine.

Looking back on the race now, the list of competitors reads like a guide to the aristocracy of the circuits. Reg Parnell (Maserati), Tony Rolt (Alfa Romeo), and Etancelin (Talbot-Lago) were all in the row behind us; and behind them sat masters like Abercassis, Bolster, Raymond Mays, Duncan Hamilton, Roy Salvadori, Bill Cotton, and many more whose names are legendary today.

The threat to the big field of Maseratis seemed to be the Talbots, driven by Chiron, Etancelin, Rosier, Giraud-Cabantous, and a Belgian newcomer called Johnny Claes. The Talbots had huge fuel tanks and could complete the 100-lap race non-stop. This meant that the Maserati drivers must use their superior speed to build up a big lead early in the race — without blowing up! But we could not afford to overlook Bob Gerard, a very steady, cool driver, who was at the wheel of a fast ERA, also with a large fuel tank. Bob's car, like our own Maseratis, always came beautifully prepared to a race.

On the day of the race we awoke to a hazy early morning but the sun broke through at noon and by two o'clock when we started our warming-up laps it was hot and clear with a blue sky but also a chilly breeze which made you shiver in the shade of the pits. Ideal weather for fast times.

Bira and I were obviously hoping for a team win, with both of us in two of the first three places. There is always tension before the start no matter how often you compete in Grand Prix racing. It is a relief when the starter's flag falls and you are able actually to start work rather than sit there on the grid worrying about the next 300 miles. Promptly at two-thirty the flag did fall and promptly the booming sounds of racing cars' revving changed to a shattering roar as the six rows of cars were unleashed.

The grid order was soon broken up with Bob Gerard shooting into the lead immediately. His advantage did not last long. Bira, driving very fast indeed as we had planned, overtook him and was soon three lengths ahead of Villoresi with Parnell, Gerard, Abercassis, and me strung behind them.

Villoresi and Bira duelled for lap after lap at, I would guess, a little under 80 mph. Gerard was plainly nursing his fast ERA, content to allow several cars to overtake him. Chiron was also taking it easily in his big-tank Talbot. After 15 laps Tony Rolt's Alfa broke a half shaft and retired. Meanwhile the Bira–Villoresi duel continued until lap 18 when Villoresi overtook Bira with Parnell only half a minute behind them and me chasing Reg's tail. Seven laps later I was aware that Bira had gained the lead again. The reason for this was soon pretty obvious. Villoresi had three pits stops. The first of these I had assumed was for fuel but shortly after resuming for the third time Villoresi retired altogether. Two of the fastest men in the race were now out of the running and I believe that Bira eased back a little, just enough to hold Reg Parnell in second place and me in third. Chiron in the Talbot was unlucky enough, as I discovered after the race, to have broken a universal in the transmission line, accounting for a dangerous jumping gear, he told me later.

I thought it wise to refuel at 36 laps and resumed the race still fighting Parnell for second place with Bira ahead of us both. Reg was, in fact, closing on Bira when he, too, had to pull in for more fuel at 43 laps. Scuderia Platé were well placed and I was beginning to feel very pleased with our team's performance when disaster struck. Bira was at the Club Corner hairpin bend when he rocketed into some bales of straw. He told me later that his brakes had failed and that after a pit inspection revealed a bent front axle he had to withdraw. It was now up to me to take the lead back for Scuderia Platé and for the next 6 laps I pursued Parnell's Maserati until I noticed that it was spilling oil on to the track. Inevitably he had to make a pit stop to improvise a plug and when he resumed the race he was in third place with Bob Gerard in second and me leading the field. At 60 laps — more than half-way through this gruelling race — I had 3 minutes over Bob Gerard. Reg Parnell was still in third place when a broken back axle forced his retirement 9 laps later.

My position was pretty good but I could not afford to relax because I knew that the steadiest man in British motor-racing, Bob Gerard, was still there in that very fast ERA. However I was cheered at one point to see that Villoresi had drifted over to my pits and was helping the pit staff with the signal board. Once he held up the single word: 'Bien.'

I was aware that Gerard was now, in fact, fading — probably more intent on finishing the race than risking a blow-up by trying to win, I thought — so I eased back to about 77 mph. I too had to nurse my Maserati. The final laps were a kind of nightmare for me. I was afraid that the motor would not hold out. My eyes were glued to the oil-pressure gauge for lap after lap.

Luck was with me however, and I won. I think that I consider this race to be my greatest for several reasons. It was my first victory in an international Grand Prix. I was the first Swiss ever

De Graffenried in his Maserati at Silverstone.

to win such a race. And it was the very first British Grand Prix. In the excitement of victory with the scream of my engines dying in my ears I realised that more than 100,000 fans had seen me win on that sunny day at Silverstone. What more could a young man wish for? I celebrated, as the saying goes, not wisely but too well at the Cornhill Hotel that summer evening in 1949. The next day I certainly knew I had joined the ranks of the few who have triumphed in an international Grand Prix. I savoured the feeling with a light heart, and a heavy head!

18

Jacky Ickx

LE MANS
1969

My finest victory? Well, first of all, it depends what a fine victory means. In the early stages of his racing career, a driver is only aware of the time-keeper's win. It is the only thing in which he is interested.

But later, when he is able to strike a distinction between merit and the result, and when he realises that they do not always go hand in hand — far from it — he comes to prefer the former to the latter. This is easily explained as a victory one has deserved, but not won, is more real than the victory won without being deserved. So it is logical for a driver to be really happy and fully satisfied with himself on some days when he has not won.

To understand this, one must distinguish victory from 'after-victory'. The latter begins the very second one crosses the finishing line. But as the change from victory to 'after-victory' is but a single step, one easily comes to identify them and consider them together while in fact they are phenomena which remain perfectly distinct.

One begins to realise this as soon as one gets accustomed to the feeling of 'after-victory'. It may even go on affording much pleasure, but one none the less realises that it is but a convention which officialises a prior triumph wherein lies the truth and reality of the victory.

At a later stage one realises that success itself is only a single expression of a personal triumph. Personal triumph is a basic requirement for success but the opposite does not hold good. It is possible to have achieved a great personal triumph and not to have it sanctioned by success. Not that this in any way detracts from the triumph or makes it less true.

Once he has seen this borne out, the driver finally places victory — the aim of his life — in the context of his personal triumph against the challenge of circumstances. Maybe he alone will know such triumph. For my part, two of my finest races were the 1969 Italian Grand Prix where I passed completely unnoticed and the 1971 Monaco Grand Prix where the Press recorded a defeat. In a word, once one has had enough experience in competition, the notion of reward becomes devoid of meaning.

Obviously, one does not disdain it when reward comes one's way; but one considers it an extra, a real gift. One learns to dissociate effort from reward, and this is why the notion of victory shifts away from the result (at best a mere officialisation of success) towards the personal triumph itself and in particular the quality of it. However, the public can only witness the official victory, so this is the kind I shall be talking about.

There are different sorts of victories. There is a whole array, and there are many levels of victory. None the less, I do not think that there can be victory without merit. Those who are against the victor endlessly intone: 'There is nothing to it with the best car!' You might as well say of Killy: 'There is nothing to it with the best skis!'

To start with, the winner has not always got the best car. And even if he has (though, how can one tell?) the drivers are so close to each other nowadays that it requires a tremendous effort to win even under favourable conditions. Naturally luck can help. One's top rival can fall victim to a failure just short of the finishing line. But to turn his ill luck to your own advantage you have to be at the right place, just behind him. And even this calls for a very praiseworthy effort.

This sort of victory, however, does not produce any real pleasure. One can never completely disregard the 'gift-from-heaven' side. For children a present is the tops; but not for adults. I myself feel that the only way to 'digest', so to speak, a victory where it has been a question of luck, is to tell oneself that this is tardy compensation for a victory one had deserved and that ill luck deprived one of.

Neither does one derive any great pleasure from the perfectly orthodox victory due to causes not directly dependent on driving. My first Grand Prix win, at Rouen, in 1968, was an example of this. A fortnight earlier we had been racing at Zandvoort where the rain had come as a surprise to everyone except myself who had not spent my youth in the country for nothing and who had felt it coming. But I was too new to the Ferrari team to demand the change of tyres, just before the start, that I considered necessary and I threw myself into the crazy undertaking of racing in a downpour with tyres which had no grip at all.

Consequently, when exactly the same situation arose in Rouen I got wet tyres fitted while all the

Ickx in the 1969 Le Mans.

others chose dry or medium tyres. But even before we reached the 'Nouveau Monde' bend the rain started to come down in torrents. Despite my being a beginner I took the lead irresistibly and won with two minutes in hand.

I should have been satisfied since that clear win was perfectly in order. I owed my lead only to my knowledge of the weather and I dare say that I had raced well, too. Still, this first Grand Prix was of little account for me although I knew that it was the first time in sixty-two years of Grand Prix racing that a Belgian had come out on top.

Then there is 'victory Jim Clark style'. Some day you find yourself with the best car, the best engine, the best tyres, and you yourself are on best form. What happens? You lead right from the start; you pull away, without resistance, your lead

increases all the time, and you reach the line in one bound. For the commentators this is splendid. They call it a 'Jim Clark victory' and they carry you shoulder-high.

They would be most surprised to hear that the driver had been deeply satisfied at *dominating* the situation but that he had felt no inner fulfilment, either during the race or after. He would have displayed his superiority and this would have meant much to him; but the race (which for him was not one) would not have afforded him what one seeks for in the sport.

Nevertheless, although one does not get full satisfaction from an easy victory showing complete superiority, a near win is not necessarily more satisfying. I am thinking, for example, of the Six Hours at Brands Hatch in 1968.

Through a masterpiece of tactics David Yorke, the number one racing-car strategist, had astoundingly succeeded in having to refuel twice instead of three times. And when Mitter's and Scarfiotti's Porsche stopped for the third time around the fifth hour I found myself with a 45-second lead.

Theoretically, this was not enough to hold off Scarfiotti for a whole hour. And yet I did manage to keep 22 seconds in hand at the finish. Needless to say it was an all-out battle. I had put my all into that last hour and was practically at limit point. I had, therefore, fully deserved the victory and yet, somehow, it failed to be a big thrill.

Why? Because I had *escaped* my rival, I had not dominated him. Winner or not, I had been the hunted, not the hunter. It is great to escape the hunter, but it is not the big thrill. Neither is it a big thrill when the win comes too early in the race.

I can remember once, for instance, at a Watkins Glen Six Hours, the first three-quarters of an hour which had been a bewildering duel between Jo Siffert and myself. I had come out the winner. But only a quarter of an hour later the Porsche gave up so that nothing threatened the victory I won. At the end of the sixth hour it was already in the far distant past. It no longer counted.

Having thus cleared the field a bit I shall now try to define what a 'fine' victory is. To my mind, the number one condition is that there should be a duel. Obviously, this is not necessarily so. What happens much more often than having a single opponent is battling with several, either all at the same time or one after another. But the pleasure of emerging from a general tussle is not quite so thrilling as when one comes out victorious from a duel.

One is, of course, glad to win and the fact of pipping one's opponent certainly adds something. But a lot is lost, too. Why? In the first place because there is not enough time to size up the battle. One has experienced it without having become actually conscious of it. And because one's adversary has not been *dominated*.

Here, however, I would like to mention how contrary is the idea of a *duel* (which the racing driver has to face) to my natural feelings. Any sport involving a confrontation between two opponents always puts me rather ill at ease because there is a *loser*. What I like about motor sport is the fact that there are none. There is a winner, obviously, but this does not make the other 19 into losers.

It is this which enables me to go in for duelling without any qualms of conscience. Even if I win, my victory won't make a loser of my opponent. Either he will come in second or he will drop out of the race and will be considered 'unlucky' . . . After these digressions we can then state the principle that, for a victor to be fully satisfied, there must be a duel and there must be no doubt as to his having won it. One's adversary must be on a par, and the conditions of the battle must have allowed the victor to give of his best.

This involves track and car, adversary and struggle, being of the same high level and one's own endeavours must be taken to the limit. At first sight, taking oneself to the limit may seem an obvious requirement for a fine victory. But what we have to realise is that no value is really absolute except as a function of one's personal level.

I can remember, ten years ago, I made this absolute effort when making my first class-win in a motor-cycling trial. And I did the same thing a few months later when I won my first beginners' race on a 50-cc. motor-cycle. Both these wins were fine victories and they still stand out clearly in my memory. Exactly the same applies to my first Cortina—Lotus victory on the Zolder circuit and to my first national championship on the same circuit. What all this adds up to is that one can witness the plenitude of victory at any stage whatever during one's sporting career. But it goes without saying that a fine victory becomes all the finer as one climbs higher in the racing hierarchy.

In today's world everyone is allowed the right to express himself, and this is without doubt a sign of progress. However, I have been astounded by the number of people who confuse this right to free expression with the right to enforce their truth upon you before acquainting themselves with the facts.

It is, for example, unbelievable that so many people should have told me that my Le Mans victory in 1969 was my finest. What I had to think about it did not appear to be of interest to them as they took no heed to inform themselves about my feelings. And very likely they would have been taken aback to have heard that I disagreed with them.

Yet their mistake is perfectly understandable as such a great stir is caused by the Le Mans race in the public mind and as television has a gift for getting the best out of a sporting event. I am sure that all those who were able to follow the final phase of the race on their television sets experienced perhaps some of the most thrilling moments in their viewing lives. I saw the film later on and even I got carried away. But seen from within things were totally different.

First of all, an endurance race is not properly a race. Moreover, the Le Mans circuit is not a driver's circuit. And again a battle between a Formula One driver and a veteran is not equal. It was luck that I was fated with a material handicap to make up for, for there is no glory in triumphing over a much older man, even if he is called Hans Hermann.

Further, the battle was brief, even though it looked as if we had been at grips for more than three hours. The suspense which held the crowd was only apparent. Finally, and this overrides all else, it was not driving but rather chess that brought me to victory in that 24 Hour Race.

At the twelfth hour, our GT40 was beaten and properly so. Elford's and Attwood's Porsche 917 was leading us by a full 8 laps and two other Porsches, two 908s, were in second and third places. The funny side of this story is that I alone refused to accept defeat. I had the unaccountable belief that the Porsches were going to disappear from the scene between the twentieth and the twenty-first hour and this boosted the team's morale when I told them. (May I just quote John Wyer in *Road and Track* with one of the finest tributes that has ever been paid to me: 'We shall miss Jacky Ickx really for his spirit. He is such a great morale-builder for the team.')

The best part of all was that my guess was right! Early in the twentieth hour the 917 slowed down and dropped out. A few minutes later it was Kauhsen's 908 which followed suit. And as Schutz's had got shunted during the night our GT40 was in the lead. But behind us there was Hermann's and Larrousse's 908 which only had one lap to make up after having been 4 laps behind, midway through the race! That meant that the 908 was gaining on us at the rate of a third of a lap an hour.

And, although it was true that we had three hours to defend our last lap's lead, we were none the less doomed to lose as we still had to refuel three times (around 10.40, around 12.15, and right at the end of the race) while the 908 was scheduled to refuel only twice more.

Despite it all I refused to give up. It was my hope that I would neutralise our opponent through personal effort. I rushed over to David Yorke to persuade him to let me keep the wheel

Ickx's GT40 during the 24-hour Le Mans race.

until the end of the race. I hasten to add that he willingly agreed. But what David Yorke contributed to my plan was the idea that actually made it a success. Since in any case we had to refuel once more he decided to do so at once. When the Porsche stopped I would do the same thing in order to synchronise operations, thus enabling us to keep our opponent under closer control. More important still, David also decided to take advantage of this unavoidable stop to change the brake pads in order to give me a sure tool for the eventual battle over the last laps.

So I got back to the wheel at 10.43.18.8 (according to the notes David Yorke took, and he is a punctilious man). I covered 7 laps and pulled into the pits some 30 seconds after the Porsche 908 had left its own pits after having refuelled for the last but one time. When I was to set off again, with the 908 on the same lap, each lap would show exactly how much lead I still had left.

But what David Yorke had not planned for was that our pit stop at 11.10 was to show up a break in an exhaust pipe which needed to be skilfully held in place with a piece of wire, thus taking our stop up to 3 minutes 8 seconds, which meant that when I got back on the track at 11.13.10.6, my lead had been reduced to a mere 10 seconds over the Porsche at that time being driven by Larousse!

What could we do? There was no question of standing out against the 908. For, although it was perhaps not so fast as earlier in the race, it was still much faster than the GT40 — both flat out and on average.

Television viewers saw this thirty times: If I came out in the lead from the Mulsanne straight, I gained 150 yards on the Porsche over the winding stretch of the circuit, i.e. up to the main stand; then it was level pegging through the less sinuous part leading to the Tertre Rouge; and, as

soon as we got to the Hunaudieres, it irresistibly caught up with the GT40 which it overtook on every lap half-way along the straight. If I had not each time leapt into his slipstream, it would probably have gained another 150 yards over me before Mulsanne.

This in the final analysis meant that, partly through my driving and partly through slipstreaming, I had to make up 300 yards a lap. And, even if this does not involve Grand Prix driving, it is still no mean affair. Besides, it is of interest to point out that although our overall average (both for the 908 and the GT40) worked out at 128·5 mph at the twenty-first hour, the average for the last three hours had been 136·1 mph. Even for the Porsche, this was pretty good going if it is remembered that Siffert, who was right in the lead at the third hour, was not exceeding an average of 137·3 mph at that time. But for the GT40, whose best practice lap had not been much faster, it was, I hope I may say, pretty impressive.

What these figures clearly show is that it was not really possible to force a win or even to get to grips with our opponent. The only possibility that lay before me was to keep close and checkmate my way to victory. It was not dice, it was not even poker, it was chess.

As long as Larousse stayed at the wheel, my only concern was to stay the pace and remain in front of him. Why? Because, as long as it was not him I was to face in the decisive phase, his driving was of no interest to me. But, when Hermann came back on the track around 12.40, I began to mosquito him, now in front, now behind, so as to observe him and feel him out on every part of the circuit.

What I must make clear at once is that harrying him in such a way, and even more so driving door-handle to door-handle in the last hour, would only have been possible with a friend. When the

Ickx winning the 1969 Le Mans.

public sees a bitter fight like this, it readily thinks of it as a show of animosity. In fact, it is quite the contrary; it is only the friendship between rivals which makes such daring possible.

One only dares what one dares when one is sure that the rival will not put one in danger. The great thing about the finale at Le Mans was that I could put my full trust in Hans Hermann. Having said that, my experience over each lap showed me that, if I came out in the lead from the Hunaudieres straight, I could not fail to win. It also proved that I came out first nearly every time if I moved out to overtake under braking. (Remember I had new brake pads.) However, we still had to see how I would manage if at the decisive time Hermann succeeded in remaining in the lead. So I purposely stayed behind him at one moment in order to apply the classical tactic of lagging behind in order to be able to take the Maison-Blanche bend faster than him and then try to cut in under braking before the Ford chicane.

What I first of all learnt during each successive experiment was that, in order to get out of the Maison-Blanche bend at the required speed, I had to begin my sprint at Arnage. On my speed out of Arnage depended the outcome of my manoeuvre $1\frac{1}{4}$ miles farther on!

I managed to pull it off the first time. On the next lap I again lagged behind and repeated the trick with as much ease. I then knew that, mechanical trouble apart, I was going to win. The final laps were hardly more than a formality. I just had to keep my eyes open . . .

There was just one funny thing: under the effect of the emotion perhaps, my Mulsanne pit completely stopped signalling to me and it was from the Porsche's signals to Hermann that I saw when the time to attack had come . . .

There are those who are fond of Le Mans and those who are not; but no one despises the triumph reserved for the winner, a triumph unrivalled elsewhere. So, I am still happy to have won the 1969 24 Hour Race at Le Mans, but this tactical victory will never be what I should call a fine victory.

What sticks in my mind after the finale which kept the crowd gasping are the 53 laps I drove in succession at practically my best practice speed, at the end of a 24 Hour Race, on a circuit which had become extremely slippery, and without ever having exceeded the authorised 6000 revs. It was a long time, 3 hours and 20 minutes under those conditions . . .

But with all this I still have not said what my finest victory was . . . Yet I imagine that with all I have said here already: that there should be a duel; that the duel should result in a clear win; that there should be an opponent of equal or higher calibre; that the conditions of the battle — circuit and formula — should provide the opportunity to give of one's best; I think you can guess for yourself . . .

19
Stirling Moss

MILLE MIGLIA
1955

Which *was* your greatest race? This is one of the questions which every racing driver finds himself being asked at frequent intervals; and it's one of the most difficult of all to answer truthfully. How do you decide? Is it the race where you won your most convincing victory? Or is it the one where you drove your best, even though you didn't win? Is it the race where luck was on your side, or the one where everything went wrong? Is it your first race, or your last, or one of the hundreds in between?

I don't know how other drivers decide, but for me there is one race out of all the events I entered which gives me the greatest pleasure to look back on. Some of the reasons are obvious enough, if you look in the record books: it was a classic race,

Stirling Moss and his navigator Jenkinson pass
through the town of Peschiera during the 1955
Mille Miglia.

with a reputation as one of the most difficult and dangerous events on the calendar. But the reasons which make it stand out in my memory are the more personal and less obvious ones. We accepted it as the challenge it was, sparing no efforts in thinking and planning to get every detail right that we possibly could. I was driving for Mercedes at the time, and in the truest sense of the words, it was a team effort. The racing organisation was an outfit where no task, however long, difficult or expensive, would ever be spared if it might conceivably make the driver's job a little easier. Beside me in the car I had Denis Jenkinson, writer, racing expert and one-time world-champion motor-cycle sidecar racer. And the race I'm talking about? It was the 1955 Mille Miglia.

Just think for a moment what kind of race it was. A fraction short of a thousand miles, over public roads lined with wildly enthusiastic crowds, with every kind of difficulty from tramlines and bumpy pavé in city centres to processions of crazy hairpins over mountain passes. An enormous field ranging from bubble cars to the latest and fastest Masaratis and Ferraris, all let loose at minute intervals for hour after hour: the slower cars were just another hazard, mobile instead of stationary, but the local boys in the really fast machinery were what we had to beat. Only Rudolf Caracciola, driving a Mercedes in 1931, had ever beaten the Italian drivers, and most people thought his feat would never be repeated. You can't hope to drive fast enough to win a race unless you know which way the road turns at every bend or over the top of every hill — if you go slowly enough to be able to change your mind, then someone who knows the road will beat you every time. That's why racing drivers have to learn every detail of every circuit — but how could anyone hope to learn a thousand miles of road half as well as drivers like Taruffi,

who drove along part of the Mille Miglia route nearly every working day of his life?

There was only one way we could make up for our disadvantages. The rules allowed two people to a car, although most drivers went alone to save weight. What we needed was a two-man team — not driver and co-driver, but driver and navigator. Yet where could we find someone who could sit there at 170 mph plus and stay cool and calm enough to give the driver the right information knowing that the slightest mistake could mean disaster? This was where Denis Jenkinson came in: anyone with his experience of sidecar racing is used to speed, racing speeds, and to relying absolutely on someone else's driving. But how could anyone with even Jenkinson's experience and knowledge of motor-racing hope to memorise every bend, every hill and every junction?

The answer we developed was the one now used by every rally driver: a set of pace notes. We even got a mention in the Guinness Book of Motoring Facts and Feats as the first to use the idea! On an 18-foot roll of paper, Denis Jenkinson wrote down the details of every section of the road — bends were classified as safe, fast, medium, slow, and very slow, and sections with bad bumps or tramlines or level crossings were all marked too. All these details were keyed to landmarks, from kilometre stones to conspicuous houses or road junctions, so we would know exactly where we were all the time. And since you can't hope to hold a conversation in an open sports-racing car going flat out, we worked out a series of hand signals, so that he could tell me exactly what was coming next: a certain wave of his hand would mean right-hand bend, moderately fast, flat out in third gear, then straight afterwards, and so on. In addition to all this, since the crowds lining the kerbs and even spilling out on to the road were such a hazard, he would have to work the linked horn and headlights too.

But the idea was only half the battle — we still had to go out on the route, which apart from the race itself was a set of public roads used by normal traffic, and find out what each and every bend was like so that we could write our notes. And this is where the Mercedes team effort came in: we went round the whole course five times in different cars. We bent one when we arrived on the same bit of road as a flock of sheep, and we crashed another when an Italian army lorry loaded with live shells turned across our path without warning. Alfred Neubauer, Mercedes' team manager, never turned a hair. Mercedes were as committed as we were, and the final result was the only one that counted.

By the time we finished our reconnaissance, we really were working as a team. Denis had enough confidence in me to say that a corner was flat-out when it was, and I had enough confidence in him to take him exactly at his word. We were taking bends at absolutely full speed, something I could never have done on my own on a road I didn't know, and going over blind brows at 170 mph, knowing exactly what lay ahead of us from the notes. But could our communications system stand up under the strain of racing against drivers who carried all this kind of knowledge inside their own heads?

At last we arrived at the starting line at Brescia, just outside Milan, in the early hours of the morning of 1 May 1955. There were four cars in the Mercedes team, the other three being driven by Hermann, Kling, and Fangio. Our car was numbered 722 in the entry list, our starting time being 22 minutes past seven. Thirty seconds before the signal we started up, and when the flag finally dropped, we roared off down the road with a full 300 horsepower at our backs. Now at last we

could see whether all the planning and all the practice had been worthwhile.

The first bend we came to was an S-bend, and while approaching it you hadn't a hope of seeing more than a hundred yards round the corner. Denis gave me the signal: flat out in fourth gear. I shifted into fourth and opened the throttle, and through we went. From then on it became almost routine. For each hazard a check of the notes, then the signal, then the action, and then on to the next. Slowly at first, the miles began to tick away, with no sign of the hundreds of other entrants, either ahead or behind. How well were we doing? Then at last, after ten miles of driving, we saw our first car ahead — one of the slower entries who had started before us. We roared past and settled down to watch for the next.

By the time we reached Verona, we were beginning to catch up on gaggles of slower cars. We passed a whole series of Austin-Healeys on the stretch leading to Vicenza, but, although we didn't yet realise it, our own turn was coming. We were making good time after an hour and a quarter's driving, when I saw in the mirror a red car overhauling us. It was no. 723, Eugenio Castellotti, in the big 4·4 litre Ferrari, driving at the absolute limit — having started next behind us, he had gained a whole minute, and was now trying to get past. We shot down the main street of the town, but with Castellotti right on my tail, I found myself approaching the next bend too fast for comfort. I had to stand on the brakes until the very last minute to lose enough speed to get around the corner. We slid across the road and bounced off the bales as I dropped into bottom gear to accelerate away but for a top-class driver that was enough — Castellotti edged past on the inside and was away like a rocket. He was trying everything he knew, showering dust and gravel everywhere as he bounced off the kerbstones. We managed to

Moss in his 3½-litre Mercedes during the 1955
Mille Miglia.

The crowd cheering Moss's great victory in the
Mille Miglia.

close up to him once, but we couldn't hold him. In a cloud of dust and burning rubber, he was pulling steadily away.

Through Rovigo we went, and along the banks of the River Po, over the bridge and through the traffic lights into Ferrara — mile after mile blurred past, until we were approaching Ravenna and the first control. We slowed up to less than walking pace, without coming to a dead stop, for cards to be checked and stamped, and collected two bits of very good news. We had broken the record time for this first stage — Castellotti had done even better, but at the price of having to drop out of the race with tyre trouble!

On we went, through Forli and then south-east, straight into the rising sun towards Rimini and the Adriatic coast. Poor Denis was finding the heat, the glare, the strain, and the noise too much for him, and he turned sideways to be sick — the 150-mph slipstream whipped his glasses away as clean as a whistle, which could have been disaster for us. Fortunately, he had another pair in his pocket, and he went on with his notes without missing a signal.

Slowly the sun climbed higher in the sky as our route took us through Pesaro, past several of the smaller, slower cars and one or two crashes by the roadside. We made for a short cut around a level-crossing marked in our notes to find it was blocked by straw bales — too late to change our minds, we had to drive right over them, and fortunately hit nothing more solid on the way through.

Pescara was the second control and the first pit stop. Neubauer had 84 men positioned around the route, working like well-drilled Trojans. They cleaned the dead flies off the screen, poured 18 gallons of fuel into the tank, handed over coffee, chocolate, and peeled bananas and sent us on our way in just 28 seconds!

Pescara saw our second short cut through the straw bales — another car swung in front of us and in avoiding him I locked the wheels, so that we crashed right through the straw barrier — fortunately we were able to carry on along the pavement and pass him before crashing back through the bales on to the road again.

By the next control, at L'Aguila, we were told that Taruffi, called by his Italian fans 'The King of the Mountains', was 18 seconds ahead of us, and the zig-zag drop down to Rome was the part of the course which he knew best. Still, we were determined to make him fight for his lead, and we kept going as hard as we could — we hit one level crossing so hard that we were both flung right up into the slipstream with the shock. We managed to pass Musso's Maserati and Maglioli's Ferrari on this stretch, but on the last lap into Rome it began to seem as if the entire population of Italy was beginning to edge into the middle of the road to get a really close-up view of the race. All we could do was swerve from side to side, horn blaring, and headlamps blazing, as if the car was out of control — it widened the ranks a little bit, but bodies were still too close for comfort as we pulled up at the control after almost $3\frac{1}{2}$ hours driving, at an average of 107 mph.

This was the first time the engine had been stopped since the start of the race. Before we could climb out, Mercedes' devoted pit-team had the car up on jacks, the rear wheels were being changed, and 60 gallons of petrol were pouring into the tanks. Someone came up with an information slip: 'Moss, Taruffi, Kling, Fangio' it read — we had done it, beaten the Mountain King on his home ground by nearly two minutes.

The whole stop took less than a minute, and we were off again. Two bends down the road, and we passed another Mercedes 300SLR, wrecked at the side of the road — it was Karl Kling who had started twenty-one minutes ahead of us. A spectator waved an upraised thumb to show he was all right — we heard later he had escaped with broken ribs.

Now we were trying to fight another tradition. 'He who leads at Rome never leads at Brescia,' said the Mille Miglia veterans — here we were, the leaders at Rome — could we still be leading at the Brescia finishing line? We were on the northward stretch towards Viterbo now, flying over hummocks and hump-backed bridges at top speed.

Then we hit one bump which we must have under-estimated — I felt the road shocks through the steering wheel suddenly cease, just as the vibration in an aeroplane stops at the instant of takeoff. Denis and I had time to look at one another — in some surprise — before we touched down again. Fortunately, although we were probably airborne for a good 200 feet, the road was dead straight at this point, and the car touched down in a perfect four-point landing!

The Mercedes team manager Uhlenhaut congratulates Jenkinson and Moss after the race.

In spite of the hundreds of bends and all the signals he had to make, Denis only missed one signal — and this was because, having been showered with petrol from an overfilled tank, he was trying to make sure the fumes were blowing clear of the hot exhaust, otherwise he and the car might have gone up like a torch!

We had another narrow escape when a front wheel locked under heavy braking and we slid into a roadside ditch — happily we were able to crawl out in bottom gear and get back into the race with nothing more than a dented tail. We passed Fangio, stopped temporarily with a broken fuel-injection pipe, and we went through the Siena control so quickly that we found out nothing about our position.

In those circumstances there was only one thing we could do — press on as fast as possible — through the Firenze control and up and over the high passes through the Apennine Mountains — the Futa and the Raticosa. Here the road was so slippery with oil and rubber we had to ease off a little in the interests of staying on the road. Poor Hans Hermann, in the fourth of the works Mercedes, was sitting at the roadside with a split petrol tank — but where was Taruffi?

The run down into Bologna was slower than we hoped, thanks to the slippery roads, so there was no time to stop and make inquiries at the control. Back down on the Emilian plain, the heat really began to build up through the afternoon — here the road was easier, straight and flat, where we could let the car rip to 177 mph in fifth along the stretches into Modena and on to Reggio. At times we were flying so fast that a light aeroplane which was following the route couldn't keep up with us.

This was really one of the most dangerous parts of the race — fatigue and over-confidence could easily make one's judgment relax until you woke up entering a corner 20 mph too fast. We had one anxious moment when the car slid sideways on a patch of melted tar, and we managed to avoid spreading it along a concrete wall by a matter of an inch or two — another came when, with the glare and the dust in our eyes, we hit a gaggle of slower cars doing a mere 110 or so. Fortunately Denis's horn-and-lights symphony got the message through in time.

We finished in fine style — round the last corner to the finishing line with the power full on, crossing the line at well over 100 mph. Yet this is where the deadening sensation of anticlimax really hit us. This was my fourth Mille Miglia, and the only one I had ever finished. But had we won, or not? Slowly we drove around to the team's garages. We had to wait until the news came through that Taruffi had dropped out with a broken oil pipe, and that no one else could possibly beat our record time. We had done it! It was an absolutely unforgettable moment, and even afterwards I found I couldn't unwind from the tension and the reaction of the drive and our victory. In the end I stayed for the celebration dinner with the rest of the team, and then finished the day by driving north through the night, over the Alps to Cologne, because I knew sleep was hopeless. Even now, so many years afterwards, the memory is fresh — of all the races I entered, and finished, and even of those I won, I can't find another to compare with it.

20
Emerson Fittipaldi

ARGENTINE GRAND PRIX 1973

Before the 1973 Argentine Grand Prix, I knew exactly how a world champion in any sport must feel. A lot of other people want to have a crack at the champion and I was very much in the firing line when I prepared for this important race in Buenos Aires.

This was to be my first race since becoming world champion and for me it was the most fiercely competitive contest I have ever entered. It was important to me because there were at least ten thousand of my Brazilian countrymen in Buenos Aires for the race and, anyway, the whole sub-continent wanted a South American victory in a field which included Europe's finest drivers. I felt all these pressures on me under the extremely hot sun of Argentina. And how hot the sun was! We

Fittipaldi during the 1973 Argentine Grand Prix.

sweltered between practice laps at the autodrome on the outskirts of the city. Peter Lyon invented a slogan as he soaked up the sun. 'The aires,' he said, 'are buenos.' But most of us needed a cool breeze!

To add to the drama of the occasion there were some very tough security precautions for drivers because there had been one of those frequent scares that one of us would be kidnapped to help further the cause of some political gangsters. No matter! The race had to go on and soon we forgot about our value to South American politics and concentrated on the business of trying for the foremost position on the grid. I was very pleased with the performance of my John Player Special. My team-mate Ronnie Peterson's JPS had gearbox troubles, but despite this he managed to gain a good place on the starting grid just behind me.

Jackie Stewart and I were burning up some fast times during practice but we could not match the fast lap time of the Swiss driver Clay Regazzoni in a BRM who got the pole position with a time of 1 minute 10·4 seconds. My own time was second fastest with Stewart (Tyrrell Ford), Ickx (in a Ferrari), Cevert (Tyrrell), Peterson (JPS), Hulme (McLaren), and Beltoise (BRM) following immediately behind us. There were 19 starters in the race which was over 96 laps, each lap being 2·121 miles and the whole race covering 203 miles. There were 100,000 spectators to watch every one of those laps and they certainly had their money's worth. For as it turned out there was hardly more than a few seconds between the leaders throughout the whole of the gruelling 200-mile epic. It must have been a great race to watch and I can honestly say that it turned out to be the most difficult race of my career.

At four-thirty the starter's flag fell and immediately the grid order was upset by Cevert who made a sensational start from the third row back and shot into the lead. Regazzoni took back the lead almost at once at the first of the two sharp corners. Cevert was second with Ronnie and I following in the team JPS's, Beltoise in fifth place, Ickx sixth, Hulme (McLaren) seventh, and Jackie Stewart's Tyrrell trailing at number eight. My policy at this stage of the race was to drive carefully, not to use too much accelerator out of the slow corners because, with tanks heavy with petrol, and a road you could fry eggs on, the tyres would become very over heated. For the first 10 laps there were hardly any changes of position except that Jackie Stewart overtook a couple of cars to become a more threatening and therefore a more interesting opponent. The leaders were nose to tail with the leader Regazzoni, the only driver able to put a little daylight between his vehicle and the rest of the pack. He held off opposition until lap 29 when I believe he found his Marlboro-BRM difficult to handle because its tyres lost their adhesion due to the overheating I had been trying so hard to avoid on my own. Finally he surrendered the lead to Cevert. I saw that the very determined Stewart had moved up to second place leaving me the chance to take Regazzoni by the 34th lap. My team-mate Peterson also passed Regazzoni and at this stage the leading drivers were Cevert, Stewart, myself, Peterson, and Regazzoni.

My duel was with Jackie Stewart who is a dogged driver, immensely difficult to pass. It was infuriating to be never more than a split second behind him and yet to be kept in my place on stretches of the circuit where I knew that I could make faster time than he. I had chosen a hairpin bend near the middle of the circuit as a likely place to overtake him. The hairpin is immediately after a very fast right-hand corner which we were taking at about 260 km/h. But it was impossible to slipstream Jackie with any success. I could not hug

his tail. The John Player Special lost all the influence of the air on its spoilers and the car began to understeer. Perhaps you can imagine what it means to slide with the front wheels, at about 160 mph! For lap after lap I tried to take Jackie on that right-hand bend. Sometimes I even shook my fist at him to tell him he was braking me! But still the laps piled up and still that wall stood between me and a crack at the leader. Cevert.

Fifty, 60 and finally 70 laps went by before I took a vital decision. I would brake very late, I mean very, very late, on the right-hand bend. I held on, screaming into the corner, watching it race towards me and finally I touched the anchors and managed to squeeze past Jackie on the inside. Jackie had been trying to close the gap between himself and François Cevert and told me after the race that he did not believe my John Player Special could possibly have achieved the speed it did after it passed him. Once I had got Jackie out of the way it was no longer a question of playing a waiting game: just to get as much speed as possible out of the JPS to make up the distance between me and the leader before planning another strike. In fact during the next 6 laps up to 76 laps I clocked the fastest lap of the race after passing Jackie. The supreme effort of the engine paid off and again I found myself having to solve the same problems that I had met behind Stewart's Tyrrell Ford. Cevert, driving the same car, could certainly open up on the straight; I could not stay too close to him on the very fast corners but in the middle of the circuit I had some advantage because I could drive quicker on these corners and brake a little later.

Tactically I would have preferred to concentrate again on the corner where I had taken Stewart. But this was now impossible. Cevert was safe from that stratagem because Jean-Pierre Beltoise in his Marlboro-BRM had spilled oil all over the circuit at this point and all of us were having to keep to the inside of the track. I was almost sure at this stage of the race that I would have to settle for second place as I roared round the circuit in Cevert's slipstream; second place in my first race

as world champion. There were only 10 laps left and when I came out of the tight right-hand Toboggan corner just before the pits I was very close indeed to Cevert. I was braking very late and with a twitch of the steering wheel I got my nose on the inside of his blue Tyrrell. Cevert came more and more over to the right, trying desperately to close me out, but I scraped through with two right-hand wheels over the green. I had made it! And the remaining 10 laps had merely to be driven fast without mistakes. With the sight of the chequered flag in my mind I drove ahead into an open road and crossed the line a clear 4 seconds ahead of Cevert and 30 seconds ahead of Stewart.

It was certainly the most difficult race of my life; the cars and drivers were so evenly matched at the head of the field. I am proud to have won in such company.

Fittipaldi leading during the 1973 Argentine
Grand Prix.